Evangelicals at an Impasse

TRINITY COLLEGE LIBRARY
Does Not necessarily approve of the
views expressed

90 $ 6.95 X

Evangelicals at an Impasse

Biblical Authority in Practice

by
Robert K. Johnston

JOHN KNOX PRESS
ATLANTA

Library of Congress Cataloging in Publication Data

Johnston, Robert K   1945–
   Evangelicals at an impasse.

   Includes bibliographical references.
   1. Evangelicalism. I. Title.
BR1640.J63   261.8   78-71048
ISBN 0–8042–2038–7

*To
Elizabeth
in the hope that she may
grow up to find the
evangelical church dynamic
and strong*

Preface

As I complete this manuscript, the United Presbyterian Church is concluding proceedings at the 190th governing assembly in San Diego, California. At this meeting, the issue of the ordination of practicing homosexuals has been debated. Rejecting the recommendation of a task-force study that such ordination be allowed, the assembly voted instead that only repentant homosexuals who choose celibacy or seek a reorientation of their sexual desires should be considered as qualified candidates for ministry. The decision is both traditional (homosexual activity is judged sinful) and groundbreaking (homosexual orientation, though a sign of the brokenness of God's world, does not disqualify a ministerial candidate). It is one further step in the continuing theological task of the wider Christian church.

Whether evangelicals will judge the Presbyterians' solution to be adequate in this case remains to be seen. Certainly it will be of wide influence. But the action of this church's governing council does point out the ever-changing body of opinion with which present-day theologians must deal. Their task is of necessity ongoing.

In the chapters that follow, there will be detailed analysis of the current debate within evangelical circles over inspiration, women's role in the church and family, social ethics, and homosexuality. As the Presbyterian decision illustrates, my discussion is, in one sense, already "dated." Such is a necessary limitation of all who seek to interact in print with the contemporary debate. Nevertheless, readers should find this discussion of evangelical opinion representative of continuing approaches to the issues.

Beyond my desire to address specific theological issues and to suggest directions in which evangelicals might profitably move, I have attempted to give voice in this book to a more basic and persistent concern. That evangelicals, all claiming a common Biblical norm, are reaching contradictory theological formulations on many of the major issues they are addressing suggests the problematic nature of their present understanding of theological interpretation. To argue that the Bible is authoritative, but to be unable to come to anything like agreement on what it says (even with those who share an evangelical commitment), is self-defeating. It is this belief which has served as an organizing principle in my writing. It is, I trust, this realization which will also make this study of more lasting value, both among evangelicals and among those seeking to learn from them in the wider Christian fellowship.

The third chapter, which addresses the topic of women, was first written in somewhat altered form as an essay in honor of one of my former teachers, Everett F. Harrison. In its original form, it was published in the Harrison Festschrift entitled *Scripture, Tradition, and Interpretation*. The fourth chapter, on social ethics, was first prepared for the National Institute of Campus Ministries' consultation on evangelical-ecumenical dialogue, held in Memphis in March 1977. It was while working on that project that I realized the underlying interpretive issue which evangelicals must broadly face. The thesis of the book evolved in this way from the middle outward. The topic of inspiration (chapter II) was chosen because it continues to be *the* most debated issue in evangelicalism (cf. Kenneth Kantzer, ed., *Evangelical Roots* [Nashville: Nelson, 1978]). Homosexuality (chapter V) was dealt with because it is perhaps the emerging issue among evangelicals.

In the process of working through these particular topics of current interest among evangelicals, I noted that each had a differing locus of theological interest. While debate over the understanding of Biblical interpretation lies at the heart of current evangelical discussions concerning women, differences in theological tradition lie at the center of discussions over social ethics, and disagreement over one's approach toward the wider secular culture is surfacing as the focus of controversy regarding homosexuality. Certainly input from Scripture, tradition, and contemporary culture remain necessary to each topic that is addressed. But one or another of these resources can be the center of theological interest on any given topic. Here is a second organizing principle around which this book has been written.

This book has been a pleasure to work on, largely because of the kindly assistance I have received along the way. Elizabeth Nordquist, who has headed the southwest chapter of the Evangelical Women's Caucus, offered valuable suggestions, as did Mary Ellen Godfrey, who holds to a more traditional posture concerning women's roles. David Hubbard (of Fuller Theological Seminary) and Donald Tinder (of *Christianity Today*) both read portions of the manuscript in an attempt to help me eliminate unintended bias in my description of contemporary evangelical positions. Letha Scanzoni was generous with her time, her knowledge, and her bibliographic resources. Don Williams and Ralph Blair were similarly generous in sharing with me their writings, whether already published or in manuscript form. For the chapter on social ethics, I benefited from the personal reactions of James Daane and of Ronald Nash, gentlemen who come to very different conclusions on the matter.

Closer to home, I am indebted to Western Kentucky University for granting me a teaching-load reduction in order that the manuscript could be completed on time. Several of my undergraduate and graduate students provided valuable assistance with research and suggestions. Alan Dunn, Paul Martin, Barbara Antonetti Davis, Ron Nutter, Phyllis Alsdurf, and John DeLautre deserve particular mention. My colleagues Arvin Vos, Robert Roberts, Robert Mounce, and James Spiceland offered substantial corrections, helping me to sharpen my discussion, as did my wife, Anne. Finally, thanks are due to Gena Porto and Brenda Lane who typed the manuscript, and to my editor, Richard Ray, who could not have been more cooperative.

June 1978
Western Kentucky University

Contents

I

The Nature
of the Impasse

Evangelicalism is currently thriving. Its churches are growing faster than their liberal counterparts; its seminaries have expanded to the point of overflow; its liberal arts colleges are successfully fighting the otherwise national trend toward insolvency; its books are widely read. People are taking note of evangelicals in a way that has not been the case heretofore in this century. *Newsweek* even dubbed 1976 "the year of the evangelical," and *Time* gave the evangelicals its cover story in the December 26, 1977 issue. For evangelicals, these are heady days.

But evangelicalism is also in a time of crisis. Recently retired *Christianity Today* editor Harold Lindsell, in his much publicized book *The Battle for the Bible,* chronicles certain of the tensions presently shaking the evangelical world.[1] He would have us know that many "evangelicals" have forfeited their right to use that title any longer. For within such diverse but traditionally orthodox groups as the Missouri Synod Lutherans, the Southern Baptists, the Evangelical Covenant Church, Fuller Theological Seminary, and the Evangelical Theological Society, there are those who no longer hold to Scripture's inerrancy. I will analyze Lindsell's definition of evangelicalism and deal with his defense of inerrancy at some length in chapter II. Here, however, it is enough to note Lindsell's contention that American evangelicalism is at a watershed in its history.

Carl F. H. Henry's recent volume, *Evangelicals in Search of Identity,* contains a more thoughtful and more tentative diagnosis of the crisis. The jacket of his book suggestively pictures a lion caught in a

maze. Given the mounting tensions and internal disunity in the orthodox camp, the evangelical movement has become for Henry "a lion
on the loose that no one today seriously fears."[2] The diversity which
Henry, as one of modern evangelicalism's founders, laments has been
noted more positively by Richard Quebedeaux in his book *The Young
Evangelicals: Revolution in Orthodoxy*.[3] In this book Quebedeaux
offers a typology for the conservative wing of the Protestant church,
differentiating Separatist Fundamentalism (Bob Jones University,
Carl McIntire) from Open Fundamentalism (Biola College, Hal Lind-
sey), Establishment Evangelicalism (*Christianity Today*, Billy Graham) from the New Evangelicalism (Fuller Theological Seminary,
Mark Hatfield), and all of these from the Charismatic Movement
which cuts into orthodox, as well as ecumenical liberal and Roman
Catholic constituencies.

In their own separate ways, Lindsell, Henry, and Quebedeaux give
common witness to the growing division on every front. Lindsell's
focus on "inerrancy" spotlights the most persistent example of conflict. But contemporary evangelicals also seem to be a house divided
on other theological issues they address—consider their discussion on
the role of women, their definitions of social ethics, and their responses to homosexuality. It is simplistic to claim as some have that
division over these other contemporary issues has arisen because of
confusion over the nature of inspiration (i. e., the inerrancy question).
No, the crisis is more fundamental. The question of inerrancy is but
one trouble spot among many. Along with social ethics, homosexuality, and women's place in the family and church, the issue of inerrancy
is essentially the question of how the evangelical is going to *do* theology while holding to Biblical authority.

Put most simply, the issue is this: how do evangelicals translate
their understanding of Biblical authority from theory into practice?
The crisis, in other words, is over basic theological method. How
does one correlate exegetical insights with an appreciation for one's
theological tradition, while remaining open to instruction from contemporary culture? Evangelicals claim to be Biblical Christians. Yet
presently they are finding it impossible to agree on what exactly the
Bible means for contemporary men and women on an increasing
spectrum of theological topics. Here is the rub.

Who Are Evangelicals?

Jesus loves me this I know,
For the Bible tells me so.
[children's hymn, Anna B. Warner][4]

In trying to delineate this crisis, it is helpful first to define evangelicalism, for the phenomenon has been variously described using psychological, sociological, and theological terms. As I use the word in this book, it refers to that group of over forty-five million Americans and millions more worldwide who believe in (1) the need for personal relationship with God through faith in the atoning work of Jesus Christ, and (2) the sole and binding authority of the Bible as God's revelation.[5] "Evangelical" is, first of all, a theological term, though its adherents may also have derivative sociological and psychological traits. The word "evangelical" distinguishes that group in Christendom whose *dedication* to the gospel is expressed in a personal faith in Christ as Lord and whose *understanding* of the gospel is defined solely by Scripture, the written Word of God. In the words of Carl Henry: "Evangelicals are to be known in the world as the bearers of good news in message and life—the good news that God offers new life on the ground of Christ's death and resurrection in the context of a biblically controlled message."[6] Evangelicals identify with the orthodox faith of the Reformers in their answers to Christianity's two fundamental questions: (1) "how is it possible for a sinner to be saved and to be reconciled to his Creator and God?" (the answer: *sola gratia, sola fide*); and (2) "by what authority do I believe what I believe and teach what I teach?" (the answer: *sola scriptura*).[7]

Biblical Authority

It is, in particular, the second of evangelicalism's two tenets, i. e., Biblical authority, that sets evangelicals off from their fellow Christians.[8] Over against those wanting to make tradition co-normative with Scripture; over against those wanting to update Christianity by conforming it to the current philosophical trends; over against those who view Biblical authority selectively and dissent from what they find unreasonable; over against those who would understand Biblical authority primarily in terms of its writers' religious sensitivity or their proximity to the primal originating events of the faith; over against those who would consider Biblical authority subjectively, stressing the effect on the reader, not the quality of the source—over against all these, evangelicals believe the Biblical text as written to be totally authoritative in all that it affirms. Although almost all Christians claim Biblical authority in some qualified sense, evangelicals posit Scripture as their *sole* authority.

Modernity's anti-authoritarian bias as well as the rise of a negative critical perspective toward Scripture has brought this evangelical claim under attack in some quarters. But, counters John R. W. Stott, to accept such a position "is neither a religious eccentricity, nor a case of discreditable obscurantism, but the good sense of Christian faith and humility. It is essentially 'Christian' because it is what Christ Himself requires of us. . . . it is Christ's view of Scripture."[9] The fact evangelicals want other Christians to face is that Jesus, the Son of God incarnate, accepted Scripture as divinely authoritative. Moreover, he not only challenged others with the absolute authority of Scripture; he also submitted wholeheartedly to it personally. Again, he commissioned apostles to teach in his name and promised them the gift of the Holy Spirit. It is these apostles who have given us the New Testament. If we are to have confidence that Christ is the bearer of the good news of the gospel, must we not also trust him in regard to his claim for the authority of Scripture?

Perhaps evangelicalism's most common argument concerning Biblical authority runs as follows: If one will grant the general reliability of the New Testament documents as verified historically, then, as the Holy Spirit uses this witness to create faith in Christ as Lord and Savior, the Christian comes to accept Jesus Christ as authoritative. Because on investigation of the text it is noted that Jesus accepted Scripture as his sole and divine authority (admittedly Jesus' pronouncements and actions were not framed in the context of the twentieth-century debate on authority, but his trust in Scripture still seems incontrovertible), Christians similarly believe the Bible to be basic to their faith and life. Moreover, Christians are given assurance of this fact by the Holy Spirit.[10]

Inspiration and Interpretation

The claim of Biblical authority stands central within evangelical theology. It is buttressed by the Scriptural corollary of Biblical inspiration. In a fundamental sense, to speak of Scripture's authority is to make a statement about God who inspired it. Seen in light of its foundations, the doctrine of Biblical authority is not first of all a statement about Scripture; it doesn't say that Scripture has this or that quality (though there are "evidences" supporting its inspiration), but that God the Holy Spirit did something—he spoke by the prophets and apostles (2 Pet. 1:21; 2 Tim. 3:16). As Geoffrey Bromiley notes, "There can be no proving of inspiration just as there can be no proving of God."[11] Rather, we dare to say Scripture is the supreme norm, for we believe that God gave it, that he attested to it in Christ, and that he uses it by his Spirit in the lives of women and men today.

Among evangelicals, the commitment to the inspiration of Scripture, a corollary to its belief in Biblical authority, has led some like Harold Lindsell and Francis Schaeffer to consider a particular formulation of the doctrine of inspiration—a belief in the inerrancy of Scripture—as synonymous with a high view of Biblical authority. Conflating Biblical authority, inspiration, and inerrancy, they have turned "inerrancy" into evangelicalism's dogmatic bench mark.[12] But to view "inerrancy" as the ground for judging evangelicalism is to reverse Biblical priorities. It is to confuse the evangelical's primary commitment to *sola scriptura* with a secondary commitment, a particular theory of the result of inspiration. "Inspiration" is that supporting Biblical tenet which grounds Scriptural authority; "inerrancy" is an inference from Biblical inspiration which many, but not all, evangelicals have traditionally supported. To make "inerrancy" the watershed of evangelicalism is to reverse the order of priority of authority, inspiration, and inerrancy. Even such spokesmen for Biblical inerrancy as Bernard Ramm, Carl Henry, and Clark Pinnock (i. e., those willing to make that inference) recognize that this is an unwise theological reduction.[13] For it is to confuse one of several possible tests of evangelical *consistency* with the test of evangelical *authenticity.*

The focus of theological discussion among evangelicals concerning Biblical authority has naturally gravitated to a consideration of the doctrines of inspiration and revelation, i. e., to a discussion of Scripture's source. The Bible's authority is God's authority.[14] Its authority is grounded in the fact that the Bible is *God's* Word. But since it is God's *Word,* an adequate concept of authority must also take cognizance of how that word is heard. The authoritative message, in other words, must not only have an adequate source in revelation; it must also be made efficacious through its reception. Scripture's authority must not only be tied to its inspiration; it must also be related to its interpretation.

Long neglected or underplayed in evangelical circles, matters of interpretation (hermeneutics) are increasingly being recognized as crucial to the maintenance of a viable evangelical doctrine of authority. As Clark Pinnock recognizes, *"The area in which a maturing of our evangelical understanding is most urgently needed is the interface between inspiration and interpretation."*[15] Pinnock is calling for the evangelical church to move beyond mere theory to the point where the Bible's sole authority actually functions to authorize theological formulation. It is the concrete working out of Biblical authority in theological matters, not its theoretical discussion, that ultimately counts. Given a lack of clarity in the interpretive process, precise refinements regarding the theoretical structure of inspiration and authority lose much of their relevance. From the doctrine of God, we must turn in our discussion of authority to the matter of Biblical hermeneutics and questions of theological formation. As Geoffrey Bromiley says, "The Bible is infallible and authoritative. But if there are different possibilities of interpretation, where is one to find that which is infallible and absolute?"[16]

It is precisely this problem that is plaguing contemporary evangelicalism. Here is its crisis. How can we translate Biblical authority into practice in our constructive theology? In a perceptive editorial in *Themelios,* an evangelical journal distributed through Inter-Varsity Christian Fellowship to theological students, Dick France bemoans the fact that evangelicals are "prone to local and changing theological fashions." Our commitment to the authority of Scripture is too often our commitment to the authority of the interpreter. He complains we do not have any adequate idea about interpreting the Bible for ourselves. "We have taught and learnt the answers rather than the method of finding them." Too many evangelicals do not know, France claims, the basic principles of Biblical interpretation.[17]

Evangelicals at an Impasse

The result is that evangelicals are currently at an impasse over the interpretation of major theological matters. "Where is it written?"—an appeal to Biblical authority—seems at present to be an inadequate basis for providing theological unity. Evangelicals, all claiming a common Biblical norm, are reaching contradictory theological formulations on many of the major issues they address—the nature of Biblical inspiration, the place of women in the church and family, the church's role in social ethics, and most recently the Christian's response to homosexuality. If evangelicals cannot discover a way to move more effectively toward theological consensus, can they still maintain in good conscience their claim to Biblical authority as a hallmark? Will their distinctive position regarding Biblical authority not die the death of a thousand qualifications?

The Adiaphora

A traditional defense by evangelicals against the charge of theological inconsistency and contradiction has been to classify all disputed theological areas as *adiaphora,* i. e., "things indifferent" to Scripture and thus of secondary importance. The claim is made that the Bible is still authoritative, for on the fundamentals of the faith—what C. S. Lewis labels "Mere Christianity"—there is unanimous judgment. It is charged that it is only among those who have not maintained the principle of *sola scriptura* that doctrinal differences on central areas of the faith have surfaced. Evangelicals might differ on forms of worship or modes of baptism, but these cannot be regarded as fundamental to the faith. John Stott quotes Richard Baxter on this point: " *'In necessariis unitas, in nonnecessariis* (or *dubiis) libertas, in omnibus caritas.'* That is 'in fundamentals unity, in non-fundamentals (or "doubtful things") liberty, in all things charity.' "[18]

But there are two problems with such a position. First, it is difficult to decide what the "fundamentals" are. Are matters of predestination, church and state, and eschatology secondary in importance and thus not to be insisted upon? Admittedly, these matters are secondary to one's understanding of Jesus as Savior, but are they secondary to the issue of Biblical authority? Are we to reduce the fundamentals of the faith to the bare bones of "Jesus is Lord"? In terms of Christian theology an affirmative answer is disastrous. Is eschatology, for example, of any less interest within Scripture than the doctrine of the authority of Scripture itself? It would be hard to support such a viewpoint Biblically. Similarly, can one's doctrine of human nature (which lies behind *all* discussion both of homosexuality and of women's place in the family and church) be considered of secondary interest within Scripture? Hardly. A similar judgment needs to be made concerning the doctrine of social ethics, and the doctrine of inspiration. As the following chapters will document, differences of opinion are surfacing within the evangelical community on these theological matters. Yet if evangelicals desire a *Biblical* faith, they must recognize that such issues are of central importance for a Biblical understanding of the Christian faith. It is not merely on peripheral issues, such as matters of church government, that we disagree.

A second problem with the *adiaphora* claim is the difficulty in defining with theological precision even those areas which relate centrally to the claim that Jesus is Lord. Well known are the disputes over the nature of the atonement. Are there allowable differences as to the nature, not the fact, of the bodily resurrection? Is Lindsell correct in his assertion that Willi Marxsen's denial of the bodily resurrection denies him the possibility of being a Christian, even though, as Beegle states, Marxsen is "absolutely convinced that Jesus of Nazareth is living and calling him to faithful service"?[19] Many evangelicals are more hesitant than Lindsell to pronounce judgment in regard to Marxsen's faith, however inconsistent they might believe his theological position to be. Matters of interpretation and theological construction are central at this point in order to arrive at a full understanding of the basic assertions of the gospel. We risk missing some of the richness of our faith as well as offending fellow Christians by pretending that interpretation is not an issue in the evangelical church.

C. S. Lewis

Paul Holmer, in his recent book on C. S. Lewis, presents an interesting variation on the *adiaphora* argument claiming that Lewis's "Mere Christianity" is not "theological" at all. Holmer writes: "Lewis moves out of the theological and out of the philosophical and into the ordinary language of everyday life." Thus, "he does not say a word calculated to help anyone to decide between denominations or rival theological views, but he does seek to get us to believe in God and Jesus Christ." He disputes the fact that "all apprehension and knowing of Christian things is via the theology or the second-level discourse."[20] It is here claimed that the issue is not one of sorting primary and secondary theological matters, but rather of sorting out and bracketing the theological issues which are secondary from primary Christian reflection. Even granting the wider intentions of Holmer's remarks (a variation of the *adiaphora* argument), they remain misleading, for they suggest it is possible to discuss Christianity nontheologically. Surely, there is a direct experience with Christ that takes place pre-critically. But matters of interpretation and theological formulation are necessarily at the heart of any *statements* about this experience of Jesus Christ.

The issue for evangelicals, in fact, finds one of its foci precisely at the point of interpreting Jesus—his attitudes toward Scripture, women, society, and so on. Moreover, Lewis's view that there is human distortion in the imprecatory Psalms, and his view that the male is authoritative over the female in church and family (because the male symbolizes God's presence) are well known and by no means universally affirmed among evangelicals.[21] They are theological judgments arising from hermeneutical considerations. Lewis would have been willing, I am sure, to admit this fact and perhaps to bracket out such issues from his "Mere Christianity." But the same hermeneutical considerations are also present in his formulations about the virgin birth, the resurrection, miracles, evil, and so on. Lewis might have been a lay theologian without formal training in certain matters, but he was, nevertheless, a *theologian*.

To reflect on issues of the Christian faith is to do theology. And it is this fact that evangelicals too begrudgingly admit. There seems to be prevalent in many evangelical circles the wishful posture that "theologies" are what non-evangelicals believe, while evangelicals accept only the "truth." Such a bias has kept evangelicals from working out their methods of theological formation and now threatens to undermine their commitment to Biblical authority as well. The matter of interpretation can no longer be ignored.

After positing the presence of *adiaphoral* issues that must be judged tolerantly, James Packer makes an interesting charge. It is also very arguable, says he, that "in each of these cases [of *adiaphora*] unexamined assumptions brought to the task of exegesis, rather than any obscurities arising from it, . . . [are] really at the root of the cleavage."[22] The trouble, in other words, is that presuppositions are too often read into Scripture rather than being read out of Scripture. Packer is surely correct on the majority of theological disputes, even within evangelicalism. Evangelicals must learn the art (science?) of theological formation so that their desire for Biblical authority can be enfleshed.

Present Theological Dangers

In the concluding chapter we will look at the nature of theological construction in light of the issues presently surfacing in the evangelical community. But prior to that discussion, a word about theological method will be helpful.

In the unfolding and presentation of Scripture's message, the evangelical interpreter must always keep God's Word central to all theological formation. Theology, that is, is a wrestling to unpack the Biblical witness. But this should not be interpreted to mean that historical-critical exegesis is alone the method of theology. For theology is more than a scientific assessment of the text; the Biblical texts must also be received as address (they are *God's* word to us) and made relevant by application (they are God's word to *us*). Such a theological program has been a constant process in the life of the church through the ages. To facilitate this process, theologians have found it necessary to bring (1) to the insights of ongoing exegesis, (2) the previous reflection of the listening church mediated through the church fathers and the church's doctrinal decisions. Moreover, (3) theologians have sought to understand the church's obligation to teach in terms of contemporary society. Thus, theology, even that theology which seeks to adhere to the principle of *sola scriptura,* becomes in practice the dynamic blending of Biblical, traditional, and contemporary sources. The Bible remains the decisive authority, but its word freshly applied and freshly experienced is only heard through exegetical, historical, and contemporary channels.

The danger of continuing to neglect matters of theological construction is that without being mindful of theology's built-in system of checks and balances, any one of the three traditional sources for theological reflection can be unintentionally absolutized, and the authority of the Word of God thus compromised. Such a threat to the vitality and integrity of the church's faith and life is discernible within the evangelical community today. Not understanding the necessary interworking of traditional, Biblical, and contemporary sources (even in a theology that seeks Biblical authority as its ultimate norm), certain evangelicals have fallen prey to a new form of "traditionalism"; others have retreated to a "Biblicism"; still others have found themselves in theological bondage to contemporary standards. An illustration of each of these errors will perhaps clarify my contention.

Clark Pinnock, in a perceptive paper entitled "The Inerrancy Debate Among the Evangelicals," warns that men like Francis Schaeffer and Harold Lindsell "tend to confuse the high view of Scripture with their own interpretation of it, so that unless one agrees with their reading of the text he may be described as an unsound evangelical or no evangelical at all."[23] Pinnock is suggesting that elements of the evangelical community are presently confusing Biblical truth with certain traditional interpretations of the Biblical record which they accept. Far from expressing genuine respect for Biblical authority, they have let an established order of religion make use of Scripture for its own purposes, albeit under the canopy of extreme respect for the text. Becoming fixed on a traditional line of interpretation, such evangelicals have removed "from God's word in Scripture [perhaps we could better say, from God's word as Scripture] its power to revolutionize the existing order."[24]

A sterilizing "formalism" is one present danger; a defensive "Biblicism" is a second. Carl Henry, in an interview on Lindsell's *The*

Battle for the Bible, charges Lindsell with having a reactionary, un-scholarly viewpoint toward Scripture in his attempt to defend its authority:

> Dr. Lindsell regards the historical-critical method as in itself an enemy of orthodox Christian faith. He seems totally un-aware that even Evangelical seminaries of which he approves are committed to historical criticism, while repudiating the arbitrary, destructive presuppositions upon which the liberal use of the method is based. Surely Dr. Lindsell does not want the seminaries to take an uncritical, unhistorical approach to the Bible![25]

But this seems exactly Lindsell's agenda. For him, questions concern-ing the dating of Daniel, the historicity of Jonah, or the authorship of Isaiah are decided doctrinally, apart from historical-critical evi-dence in the text.[26] Similarly, because of his desire to hold to a high view of Scripture, Lindsell sometimes confuses Scripture's poetic lan-guage with scientific assertion. Referring to Job 38:7, for example, which speaks of the morning stars singing together, he asserts that the book of Job is inerrant for "scientists now tell us that in the air there is music that comes from the stars."[27] Though wanting to let Scripture speak authoritatively to the church, he undercuts his intent by deny-ing a grammatical-historical method its place.

A third danger to evangelical theology brought on by inadequate reflection at the point of methodology is theology's tendency to reflect current opinion rather than Biblical truth. Without a creative dia-logue between the three components of any constructive theology, it is easy to fall into bondage to contemporary needs and concerns. Thus, the women's liberation movement in America has been compel-ling enough to some evangelicals to cause them to jettison, or at least radically qualify, Pauline authority on the subject. Virginia Mollen-kott, for example, in her article "Evangelicalism: A Feminist Perspec-tive," defines herself as a feminist, one willing "to implement the political, economic, and social equality of the sexes." She states that she has been unable to accept the "separate-but-equal double talk" of traditional evangelicalism. Thus, all the Pauline texts supporting fe-male subordination must be rejected as "the record of Paul's struggles with his rabbinic socialization" (which understood women to be inferior to men). At times Paul does not transcend this erroneous perspective in his writing, but Mollenkott believes this "does not impugn our faith in the inspiration of the New Testament."[28]

But by allowing that there is a "human element" (and by this she seems to mean a falsehood) in the divinely inspired Bible, Mollenkott has undercut her intent to let Scripture be authoritative. She has let the "good reasons" of feminism judge the Pauline texts. In chapter III we will need to look further at this issue in order to see whether an irreconcilable conflict exists between feminism and Paul's "rabbinic" texts. But whether the conflict is actual or only apparent, Mollenkott is convinced of it. Thus, rather than place the insights of contemporary society in dialogue with Scripture and tradition in a way that maintains Biblical authority, she has compromised the sole authority of Scripture by qualifying it from feminist perspectives.

Constructive Evangelical Theology

The task of theology is a risky one, but one that no longer can be neglected in the evangelical world. For God's word to be authoritative, it must function authoritatively in practice. Donald Dayton, in his review of James Barr's book *Fundamentalism*, which attacks British evangelicals' theological claims, concludes: "Without fully affirming Barr's stance, we can still hope that this book will help make clear the bankruptcy of reigning evangelical paradigms of biblical authority and thus accelerate the search for more adequate ways of conceiving the authority of the Scriptures."[29] Dayton is correct in noting the current problem in evangelicalism concerning Biblical authority, but wrong in asserting the inadequacy of evangelicalism's paradigms. It is not the theoretical underpinnings of Biblical authority that are in error, but the evangelical community's inability to translate theory into practice. It is not the notion of inspiration that is erroneous, but the inattention to matters of interpretation.

In the following chapters, I will chronicle this current impasse in evangelical theology. Chapter II will focus upon the nature of inspiration as it is presently being debated. Chapter III will concentrate on the role of women in the church and family. Chapters IV and V will highlight the divisions over notions of social ethics and homosexuality. With each issue, I will attempt to acquaint readers with the nature of the current problem by delineating the differences presently surfacing and by then clarifying the issues involved. By doing this, my hope is to point evangelicals beyond their current impasse by suggesting where new theological input is surfacing—whether from exegetical, contemporary, or traditional sources.

This book is a plea on two fronts: First, for an irenic and loving spirit within the evangelical community as controversies are debated. If the theological task cannot be carried out prayerfully and with a real sense of community, all will be the losers. If the modernist-fundamentalist controversy of our past has taught us anything, it is the tragic consequences of polarization. Second, this book is a plea for consensus-building in theological formation. Only as the evangelical church continues to strive for unity on major theological issues can it continue to claim Biblical authority as a foundational principle. Can we continue to overlook theological inconsistency, maintaining our own "party line" by the exclusion of other voices?

In the sixth and concluding chapter, we will look at this task of theological formation in some detail, seeking to learn from the contemporary discussions on theological issues that previous chapters have documented. Can the discussion on women, for example, provide the evangelical church a test case in theological construction? Can the other current issues function similarly? It is with this question in mind that I turn to address what has been evangelicalism's most persistent controversy—the nature of inspiration.

II

The Debate over Inspiration: Scripture as Reliable, Inerrant, or Infallible?

Debate over the precise implication of Scripture's inspiration has continued almost unabated within modern evangelicalism. In a poll taken by *Christianity Today* in 1957, for example, among members of the Protestant clergy who chose to call themselves conservative or fundamental, 48% affirmed that belief in Scripture's inspiration also demanded a commitment to its inerrancy, while 52% said they were either unsure of the doctrine of inerrancy or rejected it outright.[1] Discussion within evangelicalism concerning the inspiration of Scripture has usually focused on this point: whether or not Scripture is inerrant. So prominent has been this debate that outsiders have often regarded evangelicals as holding, not to a distinct view of the sole *authority* of Scripture (as was argued in the previous chapter), but to a belief in Biblical inerrancy.[2]

Reasons for the Debate

"Inerrancy" has been *the issue* among evangelicals for three reasons—one Biblical, one theological, and one sociological. *Biblically,* the issue has continued to provoke debate, for while Scripture asserts its own inspiration, it nowhere is explicit regarding the result of that inspiration. Although 2 Timothy 3:16 declares "all scripture is inspired by God" (literally, "God-breathed"—*theopneustos*), this claim is never unpacked. The text asserts that God brought Scripture into being, and that, therefore, it is profitable "for teaching, for reproof, for correction, and for training in righteousness." But what the other implications of Scripture's "God-breathedness" are, and how its divine origin correlates with its human dimension, are nowhere delineated. Similarly, 2 Peter 1:21 states that prophecy has come not by the impulse of man, "but men moved by the Holy Spirit spoke from God." Scripture's authority and trustworthiness are grounded in its God-givenness (*apo theou,* from God). But again, the precise nature of this identification of the prophet's words with God's Word is not specified.

Theologically, the debate over the significance of Scripture's inspiration has been fostered by the great importance of the subject. There are few if any areas within Christian life and thought that do not lead back to this tenet which grounds Biblical authority. The heat generated by this topic is witness to the fact that we are, in Pinnock's words, "close to the heart of the conception of religious authority in our evangelical confession, which 'limits the ground of religious authority to the Bible.' "[3] There is a "deep relationship between *origin* and *authority*" that cannot be ignored.[4] Thus discussion concerning the implications of inspiration is of interest to all evangelicals who seek to be Biblical Christians.

Sociologically, the debate has been largely American and has continued to be fueled by the memory of the modernist-fundamentalist controversy which raged between men like B. B. Warfield and Charles Augustus Briggs at the turn of the century. Perhaps for this reason, conservative theologians from both Britain and the Continent have often failed to become involved in the discussion, even misconstruing its significance because of their radically altered historical context.[5] In a recent article on evangelical identity, Gerald Sheppard goes so far as to claim that "inerrancy" is for American evangelicals "the official language of social identification, over against other so-called 'non-evangelical' institutions." It is the use, or non-use, of this word, he claims, that has provided "the most common rhetorical means by which nuances . . . [are] officially distinguished in the evangelical identity."[6] Sheppard finds evidence for this claim in the ongoing controversy at Fuller Theological Seminary, whose history parallels in many ways the rise of modern American evangelicalism. Debate at Fuller has never touched such major orthodox doctrines as the deity of Christ, the resurrection, virgin birth, or second coming. Instead, it has consistently centered on a correct interpretation of the nature of inspiration.[7]

Difficulties with the Discussion

Although the subject matter of inspiration has been judged as of crucial importance, creative theological formulations have been made difficult within American evangelicalism for at least two reasons. David Hubbard, in his article on the debate over Scripture's inspiration entitled "The Current Tensions: Is There a Way Out?", refers to "the silence of evangelical *biblical* scholars"—i. e., their reticence to publish their findings and enter into open theological dialogue. He states:

> I have a hunch that one explanation accounts for the silence of evangelical *biblical* scholars more than any other: the basic fear that their findings, as they deal with the text of Scripture, will conflict with the popular understanding of what inerrancy entails. Where a rigid system of apologetics becomes the basic definition of orthodoxy, true biblical scholarship becomes difficult if not impossible.[8]

Hubbard is echoing Edward J. Carnell, his predecessor as president of Fuller Seminary, whose book *The Case for Orthodox Theology* is perhaps the classic statement on modern evangelicalism:

> a heavy pall of fear hangs over the academic community. When a gifted professor tries to interact with the critical difficulties in the text, he is charged with disaffection, if not outright heresy.[9]

The threat of heresy also relates to a second problem in the development of a constructive theology of inspiration. It has encouraged an "apologetic" excess among all parties in the discussion, blurring the issue by selective argument and loaded terminology. On the one side, many proponents of inerrancy attempt to restrict the discussion of inspiration to the God-relatedness of Scripture, claiming with Balaam that " 'God is not man, that he should lie.' " (Num. 23:19) Overlooked along the way are questions pertaining to the meaning of error, its relationship to lying, the role of human agency, the importance of the author's intention, and so on. On the other hand, certain opponents of inerrancy have become preoccupied with the human

character of Scripture, claiming that "to err is human." Thus, the fact
that God is the ultimate author of Scripture is downplayed for apologetic reasons, the stress being instead put on the "fallible" human
minds and hands that produced the text. Such a bifurcation of the
divine-human nature of inspiration is unfortunate and confuses the
theological task. An unnecessary polarization results which paints
everyone in black-and-white terms. In fact if one were to take seriously the criticisms by both sides, one might conclude that the choice
facing evangelicals today is between doctrinal declension or shoddy
scholarship.

Recent Developments

Although the debate has been marred by the fear of being judged
heterodox on the one hand, and by apologetic excess on the other, it
has continued unabated. In September of 1977, for example, a group
of thirty prominent evangelical leaders met in Chicago to form the
International Council on Biblical Inerrancy and to map out a ten-year
effort to study and defend the doctrine. Through conferences, pastoral
training centers, traveling seminars, and technical dialogues with non-
inerrantists, the ICBI is attempting to show that those who deny
inerrancy are "out of step" with the historic evangelical mainstream
and with the Bible. Although not everyone in their organizations
would agree with their positions, leaders from such evangelical
strongholds as Inter-Varsity, Campus Crusade, Trinity Evangelical
Divinity School, *Christianity Today,* and Gordon-Conwell Seminary
signed the summary document.

Reaction to the Council has shown the deep-seated differences
within the evangelical community. Carl Henry, for example, a sup-
porter of inerrancy, declined to participate in the conference. Clark
Pinnock, another traditional advocate of inerrancy, was quoted as
saying:

> "The last thing we need is a ten-year inerrancy compaign.
> ... The phenomenon of Scripture demands more than simply
> a theory developed by the Princeton boys in the 19th century.
> ... A campaign for inerrancy will encourage people to avoid
> the real issues."[10]

Perhaps wishing not to fight the battle on hostile terrain, David Hubbard, who dislikes the term "inerrant," nevertheless responded that he welcomed the Council's formation, for " 'evangelicals should support anything that contributes to a better understanding of Scripture.' "[11] Non-inerrantist Jack Rogers countered more candidly that he resented the Council's use of the term "historic" to refer to what is in reality a "modern" notion of inerrancy.[12]

To understand the stridency of the Council's campaign, or Pinnock's vehemence, or Hubbard's circumlocution, it is necessary to describe more carefully the different approaches regarding the doctrine of inspiration of which these men are representative. Within contemporary evangelicalism, there are, at present, four distinct positions which are being taken regarding inspiration's implications. While there are permutations within these basic categories, one can distinguish the following: (1) detailed inerrancy, (2) partial infallibility, (3) irenic inerrancy, and (4) complete infallibility. Although evangelicals hold in common to Scripture's inspiration and authority, they differ over the implications of these truths. "Detailed Inerrantists" claim that a commitment to Scripture's inspiration demands that the original copies of the Bible be considered without error, factual or otherwise. "Irenic Inerrantists" agree that the Bible is without error, but believe Scripture itself must determine according to its intent the scope of that inerrancy. "Complete Infallibilists" reject "inerrancy" as a helpful term for describing the total trustworthiness of the Biblical writers' witness, substituting the word "infallible" in its place. "Partial Infallibilists" believe that the authors' intended message is in error at points, but their witness to the gospel is trustworthy and authoritative.

It is to a discussion and comparison of these four viewpoints that I now turn. Having noted basic differences in these positions, we can then look at a number of questions which evangelicals must address if they hope to move beyond the present impasse in their theological understanding of the doctrine of inspiration.

1. Detailed Inerrancy

Taking the initiative in recent discussion concerning inspiration are apologists like Francis Schaeffer and Harold Lindsell who see inerrancy as the watershed of the Christian faith. Schaeffer created much consternation among fellow evangelicals by threatening not to appear at the rostrum of the International Congress on World Evangelization which convened in July of 1974 in Lausanne, Switzerland. What was at issue was the wording of the Lausanne Covenant on the subject of Scripture. The statement, which sought to summarize the beliefs of the evangelical community, affirmed Scripture's "inspiration, *truthfulness* and authority." Omitted was the word "inerrancy," though Schaeffer was pleased with the attached explanation which asserted that Scripture was "without error in all that it affirms."

Using this subsidiary phrase to champion his position, Schaeffer published as a follow-up to the conference a pamphlet entitled *No Final Conflict: The Bible Without Error in All That It Affirms.* In this pamphlet Schaeffer states that what is "at stake is whether evangelicalism will remain evangelical." Without the entire Bible being considered "God's verbalized communication to men giving propositional true truth [!] where it touches the cosmos and history," Schaeffer believes that Christians lack an adequate authority on which to build their faith. Suspicious of the role of hermeneutics (it is a means of "explaining away the *brute factness*" of Scripture), Schaeffer considers in the booklet the Genesis 1—11 account, but without regard to its literary genre. Taking a literalistic reading of the text, he attempts to show how it can fit into a scientific understanding of the cosmos. Too often, thinks Schaeffer, Christians have tended to value the "truth of science" more than the truth of the Bible. Schaeffer seeks to reverse this ordering.[13]

Lindsell, in his book *The Battle for the Bible,* contends that the Bible itself and the history of the Christian church support a view of inspiration that insists on the inerrancy of the autographs of Scripture in every detail of chronology, geography, astronomy, measurement, and the like, even when such details are incidental to the central intent of the passage.[14] Because he believes that both the Bible and the orthodox tradition of the church support inerrancy, Lindsell feels justified in denying the term "evangelical" to those who reject this doctrine. Moreover, he views inerrancy as crucial for all of Christian theology; for without a watertight epistemological defense against liberalism, heresy will enter into the church and destroy its very faith.[15] According to Lindsell, the history of such formerly "evangeli-cal" groups as the Lutheran Church—Missouri Synod (at least the Seminex supporters), Fuller Theological Seminary, and the Southern Baptist Convention reveals that once inerrancy is abandoned, there is an inevitable, even if prolonged, deterioration of the faith. Evangelism is undercut; spiritual sterility sets in; and apostasy looms on the horizon ready for the next generation to embrace.

Lindsell's book is a work of apologetics, a polemical discussion backing up his claim that to be an evangelical demands a commitment to the notion of inerrancy. Although the term is qualified to exclude faulty grammatical construction or textual transmission, Lindsell's definition of error does include any "misstatement or something that is contrary to fact."[16] Thus, Lindsell posits that the cock crowed six times for Peter (in order to harmonize the Gospel accounts); he concludes that "about 23,500" people died on a certain single day (in order to account for Numbers 25:9 citing 24,000 as the figure while Paul asserts in 1 Corinthians 10:8 that it was 23,000); and he hypothe-sizes that the "molten sea" described in 2 Chronicles 4 as being ten cubits in diameter and thirty cubits in circumference (although we know that $C = \pi D$, i. e., the circumference of something ten cubits in diameter is actually 31.4159 cubits) can be understood if the vessel is considered to have sides that are four inches thick, and if the measure-ment for diameter is taken from the outer edges while the measure-ment of circumference is taken from the inner edge.[17]

Two problems with Schaeffer's and Lindsell's position need to be mentioned here. First, contrary to their claims, the historical back-ground for the doctrine of inerrancy is extremely complex. A modern concept of inerrancy involving scientifically precise language was of course unknown prior to the rise of modern science. Thus, even when the church fathers claim that the Bible is without error, we can be almost certain that "error" did not mean for them what it means for us today. We cannot, for example, read into Calvin our own preoccu-pations, and expect him to answer questions which are ours, not his.[18] The temptation is to line up the evidence that supports one's position and ignore conflicting statements. It is true that one can find among individual theologians support for an "inerrancy" position through-out the history of the church, but it is also true that these same theologians often exercise in their exegesis much greater freedom than Lindsell's or Schaeffer's interpretation of their theory would seem to allow.

The church corporately has been cautious in making the "inerrancy" claim normative for Christian life, using instead words like "authority," "sufficiency," and "infallibility" in its creedal pronouncements. Lindsell is perhaps the most flagrant offender, but detailed inerrantists commonly tend in their apologetic zeal to conflate such terms as "inspiration" and "infallibility" with "inerrancy." Because the church has traditionally accepted Scripture's inspiration, these inerrantists claim that "inerrancy" is also the church's historical position.[19] Such an argument must be rejected. If we place it historically, "inerrancy" finds its home most comfortably in the post-Reformation scholastic orthodoxy of a Turretini or in the nineteenth-century Princeton theology of Alexander and Hodge.

Second, detailed inerrantists rely heavily on a form of the "domino theory": reject inerrancy and one will be forced to abandon other cardinal doctrines of orthodox Christianity. Opponents are judged to hold a position of "limited errancy" (even if they deny such charges) which "can slide easily into an unlimited errancy stance."[20] Without the solid platform of inerrancy to stand upon, evangelicals will move down the gentle slope of "limited errancy" to apostasy.[21] Besides its weakness as an *ad hominem* argument, such a charge is also naive historically.[22] Fellow inerrantist John Woodbridge, for example, warns against such an "all-or-nothing mentality," for "it does not fit all the available historical data." In his article "History's 'Lessons' and Biblical Inerrancy," he points out the case of Jean Le Clerc who moved from a more critical position regarding Scripture's inspiration to a more conservative one.[23] The abandonment of inerrancy does not force one to embrace permanently liberalism and/or apostasy. In fact, one can defend a high view of Scripture without recourse to the term "inerrancy" as I shall argue in this chapter.

2. Partial Infallibility

At the other end of the evangelical spectrum from Lindsell and Schaeffer are those like Dewey Beegle and Stephen Davis who believe that one must admit there are errors in the text of Scripture, even in areas related to the author's intention.[24] Such errors, however, do not involve any of the basics of the faith. The Bible is inspired, but in a qualified sense, relating primarily to the essentials. The norm for judging what is essential is the gospel message contained therein. With regard to the gospel, the Bible as inspired still proves itself to be accurate and trustworthy, and thus authoritative.

Beegle's first book, *The Inspiration of Scripture,* proved to be the most controversial book within evangelicalism in the early sixties.[25] Published in 1963, it was given ten pages of review in *Christianity Today* by editor Carl Henry and contributing editor Frank Gaebelein. In his book Beegle attacked "inerrantists" for being overly rationalistic, obscurantist in fixing upon the "autographs" of Scripture, naive linguistically in thinking language can be precise, misguided in their use of proof-texting, Docetic in their denial of Scripture's humanness, and wrong in their commitment to a domino theory regarding inspiration. Any dangers in renouncing inerrancy were largely imaginary, Beegle claimed; one must let the "facts" of Scripture show straight forwardly what kind of book it is and that will suffice.

In a second edition of his book, renamed *Scripture, Tradition, and Infallibility,* published ten years later, Beegle attempts to broaden his discussion by including the Roman Catholic situation concerning a theology of inspiration and Scripture. He also seeks to move beyond his intended "demolition job" on inerrancy to strike a more positive note.[26] But the essential thrust of his argument remains the same. Beegle eschews a deductive methodology (one based in a doctrine of God) and proposes instead an inductive approach to the study of inspiration. Such an investigation, especially when correlated with an analysis of the process of Scripture's canonization, textual transmission, translation, and reception, suggests to Beegle that there are degrees of inspiration within the Bible. Luke's inspiration, for example, is not unique, for he is only a historian. Beegle states, "What distinguishes Luke from Christians today is not inspiration as such, but rather the unique period of revelation that he was privileged to witness." Similarly, Beegle believes that the song writers Isaac Watts and Charles Wesley, had they "lived in the preexilic centuries of David and his successors and been *no more inspired than they were in their own day,*" would no doubt have had their hymns included in the Hebrew canon. The ground of Scripture's authority is not its inspiration which dynamically extends into the present as well, but its "structure of theology, the gospel, that undergirds the whole of the Bible and in one way or another informs, and expresses itself in, each of its texts."[27]

Stephen Davis's book *The Debate About the Bible* is a response to Lindsell's attack and seeks to answer the question, "Must a person believe in inerrancy to be an evangelical?" Davis writes as a practicing philosopher with strong ties to the evangelical community. He holds the Bible to be "inspired, authoritative, trustworthy, and, as I define the term, infallible." Although the majority of his book is a refutation of Lindsell's arguments, Davis does spell out his own position as being that the Bible is "infallible, as I define that term, but not inerrant."[28]

As with Beegle, an inductive approach to inspiration is taken. Davis states that he must admit the text is in error (i. e., it has made a false statement) when it uses God to justify the murder of innocent people in the taking of Canaan, or when the book of Jude attributes the pseudepigraphic (first-century, B.C.) book of Enoch to the well-known Biblical character, or when it quotes Jesus' reference to the mustard seed as the smallest of all seeds. Though he admits he cannot absolutely prove these are errors, Davis says they seem so to him. Using a similar kind of argument, he realizes that he cannot claim *a priori* that the Bible is infallible (i. e., that it makes no false or misleading statements on matters of faith and practice); but he believes such a statement best explains the evidence he sees. Although he realizes that he cannot prove his contention and must, in fact, leave open the possibility he is wrong, Davis considers the Bible fully trustworthy on all matters that are "crucially relevant to Christian faith and practice." As a working hypothesis, "infallibility" is kept in order to affirm with the Christian tradition that the Bible as "God-breathed" has full doctrinal and moral teaching authority.[29]

Both Davis and Beegle echo the posture of P. T. Forsyth, the English theologian of the turn of the century, who said, " 'We may not feel compelled to take the whole Bible, but we must take the Bible as a whole.' "[30] That is, although specific sections of Scripture might need to be rejected, one must still take as authoritative the overall message of the Biblical text. There are problems with such a position, however, both at the point of rejecting "the whole Bible" and at the point of accepting "the Bible as a whole."

Davis is perhaps more candid than Beegle in recognizing that he cannot be dogmatic concerning what in Scripture is to be rejected. Beegle implies that modern scholarship can indeed do that and that it has therefore created a new situation today. This is, however, not true. All of the examples Beegle mentions are long-recognized difficulties in the Biblical text which have been debated by theologians throughout the centuries. Even more to the point, no two modern-day scholars seem able to draw up the same common list of errors, each finding on the other's worksheet difficulties which have, in their opinion, plausible modern-day alternate explanations often involving a reassessment of the author's intention and/or cultural context.

Second, if we accept only "the Bible as a whole," how are we to determine what is essential from what is nonessential? If error in matters of faith and practice is allowed on the periphery, as well as error in incidentals, by what criteria do we arrive at the nonnegotiable borders? Davis and Beegle propose to use as a norm their understanding of Christ and his gospel. But this is to subject Scripture to an outside criterion which the interpreter brings to the text. Rather than accepting as authoritative Scripture's total witness, the interpreter uses either his subjective experience with the Christ, or his contemporary sensibility, or the church's traditional understanding of the gospel, or perhaps some combination of these to judge what reasonably the "whole Bible" might be saying. While Scripture is still considered vital to an understanding of the faith, it is relegated to a secondary authoritative role—one factor among several. Davis, in fact, concedes this point, recognizing that his decisions regarding what to accept and what to reject are based on "good reasons" stemming not only from exegesis, but also from his total understanding of Christian theology. Here, he states, is his "imprecise and flexible" criterion for judgment.[31]

The problem for those holding to limited infallibility is this: an external criterion is used to determine the extent of inspiration. Inspiration is imputed to only the "essential" elements of the text; inner experience, church tradition, or contemporary standards of reasonableness determine what that essence is.

Ironically, external criteria are the basis of judgment for those holding to a detailed-inerrancy position as well. As is so often the case, errors at the far right and far left of any given issue end up having a surprisingly similar shape. On the far right, it is not the gospel's "essential elements" standing judge over Scripture's inspiration; instead, the "scientific accuracy" of the text gives it its ultimate verification. Demanding strictly scientific precision to guarantee Scripture's trustworthiness, requiring something more objective than the internal, personal witness of the Holy Spirit through the text itself, scholars like Lindsell end up testing the truth of the Bible by an extra-Biblical standard.[32] As with Davis, externally derived "good reasons" become the ultimate criterion for judging the gospel.

The results are unfortunate in both cases. First, since the norm for establishing the truthfulness and thus authority of Scripture is external to the Bible itself, confidence in the Bible and its message can only be highly probable. On the one hand, as Lindsell demonstrates, one's confidence hinges on being able to harmonize 23,000 with 24,000, or to correlate a diameter of ten with a circumference of thirty. One error brings the edifice crashing down. As Clark Pinnock states, one gets "the strong impression that the authority of the Bible and with it the truth of the gospel hangs on the resolution of some chronological puzzle or mechanical detail."[33] Is it really true that our confidence in Scripture's claim regarding Jesus as Lord rests on such a basis? On the other hand, the "good reasons" of Davis provide scarcely a better foundation for knowing what we should believe. Though Davis is himself quite eager to submit to the teaching authority of Scripture, he allows for the bracketing out of certain texts while canonizing others for critical-personal reasons. Moreover, he admits that he cannot prove his contentions.[34]

Second, we find in these extreme positions a compulsion to maintain one's stance—by refusing to admit error (the detailed inerrantists) or by discovering error (the infallibilists). For the inerrantist, this brings one of three results: either the evidence is transformed to conform with the theory, or the theory is inconsistently and quietly changed, or "error" is so qualified that it can never be located in practice. For example, in trying to harmonize the Gospel accounts, Lindsell feels compelled to posit that the cock crowed six times within Peter's hearing, although the various Gospel texts clearly say "three." When the data do not allow for such manipulation, as with Jesus' remark that the mustard seed is the smallest seed, then Lindsell slides into an argument that hinges on the author's intention (e. g., "it was the intention of the speaker to communicate the fact that the mustard seed was 'the smallest that his hearers were accustomed to sow' ").[35] But his commitment to scientific accuracy is thus qualified, though this is nowhere admitted. Last, for a genuine error to be acknowledged by Lindsell, it must be *indisputably* false. But with Scripture's autographs no longer extant, they are by Lindsell's criterion unfalsifiable. "Inerrancy" has become a shibboleth, to be defended even at the expense of theological discourse.

On the other side, for Beegle and Davis, pressure to defend their position (now, by locating "error") brings equally unsatisfactory results. Davis posits that the Bible is erroneous because of the variation in the parallel accounts of David's numbering of the people found in 2 Samuel 24 and 1 Chronicles 21, because the mustard seed is not the smallest seed as stated in Matthew, and because the brutality of Canaan's conquest by the Israelites could not be God-ordained as is claimed. Such "difficulties" are "errors" however, only if the context, literary genre, and purpose of the respective texts are disregarded. Adequate interpretations exist for each case that Davis raises. Beegle's methodology is scarcely better. He claims to reexamine traditional viewpoints "in the light of new information gained during the last forty years or so."[36] But tellingly, all of his examples are familiar to traditional theological discussions and have not increased in difficulty in the modern era. The problem of "errors" in the text is not a new one, and Beegle's claim in this regard seems unfounded—merely an apologetic ruse.

Both detailed inerrantists and partial infallibilists compromise Scripture's inspiration by the use of outside criteria for evaluation and judgment. Moreover, they fall prey to questionable methods of argument in their desire for apologetic effectiveness. It might be fair to say that one side is guilty of overbelief; the other, of underbelief. One side expects too little from the Biblical text; the other, too much. Both have let polemical and apologetic concerns become primary, with the result that the authority and truthfulness of the Biblical text are undermined. Rather than search among theologians such as these, we must look to the mediating categories within evangelicalism—to the irenic inerrantists and to those holding to complete infallibility—if helpful insight is to be gained.

3. Irenic Inerrancy

An increasing number of evangelicals are recognizing that the word "inerrant," when used in theological discussion, must be defined Biblically; it must be given a meaning related to standards in Biblical times. Such an attempt has taken several directions, but perhaps the views of Clark Pinnock and Daniel Fuller are most representative of this more flexible and irenical position.

Pinnock is, like Lindsell and Schaeffer, first of all an apologist, as can be seen in the titles of his books: *Set Forth Your Case, A Defense of Biblical Infallibility,* and *Biblical Revelation.* For Pinnock, the Bible authorizes and authenticates the preaching of the gospel. "To construct a theology on the basis of an unreliable Bible," he writes, "is to build on sand."[37] But this is not necessary, for Scripture's inspiration guarantees that it is infallible (i. e., it is incapable of deception) and inerrant (i. e., it is without error in all that it affirms). Read in its natural sense, Scripture is fully trustworthy in all matters that the writers affirm. States Pinnock:

> The importance of Biblical infallibility is measured by the *sola scriptura* principle, wherein the Bible is taken to be the sole source for the knowledge of divine truth. The foundation of theology is, therefore, only as secure as the Bible is trustworthy. . . . *Sola scriptura* cannot be sustained apart from Biblical infallibility. An erring standard provides no sure measure of divine truth and human error. The assurance in which the believer knows and rejoices in his Lord's nature and purposes is threatened when the reliability of Scripture is questioned.[38]

Pinnock might seem to be one with Schaeffer and Lindsell given the above (he did, in fact, spend some time studying under Schaeffer at L'Abri, Switzerland). But Pinnock adds the important qualification that Scripture's infallibility (and thus inerrancy, which he deduces) must be understood Biblically according to an adequate hermeneutic. To his deduction concerning a doctrine of inspiration, he adds an important inductive qualification.

In his earlier writing, Pinnock's Biblically derived qualifications concerning inerrancy were based on the facts that modern historiography was unknown in Biblical times, that writers use the language of simple observation (e. g., the sunrise), that figurative and mythological language is used (Isa. 27:1; Job 9:13), that parallel accounts take different standpoints (e. g., Samuel—Kings—Chronicles; Matthew—Mark—Luke—John), that Old Testament citations in the New Testament are often loosely rendered, and that literary quality varies from writer to writer. According to Pinnock, purported "errors" in the Bible often dissolved when the above observations were noted. Pinnock realized that others found "error" also due to inconsistencies in the sources Bible writers quote, moral accommodation to prevailing standards in Biblical times, scientific inaccuracies, and pseudonymous writing intended to deceive the reader. But for Pinnock these "assured results" of scholarship which allegedly crippled infallibility were "little more than the current popular hypotheses grounded upon the dubious assumption that Scripture may contain errors."[39] Remove the probability of error as one's starting point and instead substitute a "scientific" (inductive) approach to Scripture, one beginning with the Bible's own teaching concerning its infallibility, and building criticism of it from there, and even these more difficult problems dissipate.

While keeping to his general framework, Pinnock has, in more recent writing, modified his judgments on the irreconcilable differences between a high view of Biblical inspiration and such critical claims as error in the Biblical sources. He has sought better to qualify "inerrancy" inductively—according to the "scope, purpose, and genre of each passage." The author's *intention* has been given increased significance, as in the following examples which he cites:

> in confusing the facts of the Abraham story in Acts 7 we fault neither Stephen for citing the facts as he recalled them nor Luke for recording what he believed Stephen said; where Job cites the errant opinion of liars; where the chronicler recounts figures quite different from those in parallel passages, his inten-

tion being only to set forth the record as he found it in the
public archives; where the *ipsissima verba* of Jesus are handled
with a certain freedom depending on the purpose of the redac-
tor evangelist, or where Paul cites the Old Testament freely in
line with some concept he wishes to teach us.

For Pinnock, the implication of this hermeneutical qualification to the
notion of inerrancy is that though the Bible *"contains* errors" it
"teaches none."[40]

"Inerrancy," understood in this way, is "a good deal more flexible
than is supposed," according to Pinnock, "and does not suspend the
truth of the gospel upon a single detail, as is so often charged."[41]
Moreover, Pinnock's qualifications concerning Scripture's inerrancy
are internally derived and textually oriented. He is not using externally formulated theological categories like "faith and practice" or
"revelational matters" to judge a specific Scriptural text's intention,
nor the "good reasons" of the interpreter, but is rather letting each
passage declare its own scope and purpose through its own genre and
historical context.

Pinnock's flexible use of the word "inerrancy" causes him to
criticize certain evangelicals like Lindsell for an "overbelief about the
Bible" which seeks to protect it from its own humanity.[42] It compels
him to criticize the position of irenic inerrantists like Daniel Fuller,
who, according to Pinnock, operate in their judgment of Scripture's
infallibility according to an *a priori* standard derived inductively from
doctrinal verses (2 Tim. 3:15), but then applied deductively and uniformly throughout the text. It also allows him to criticize more liberal
evangelical theologians who would seemingly sacrifice the principle of
sola scriptura for another standard. Most important, Pinnock's position allows him to maintain a strong Biblical foundation for his theology, while at the same time being open to new exegetical and critical
insights. Pinnock is willing to make a strong apologia for *sola scriptura* and to criticize alternate viewpoints. But he also urges "charity
toward those whose hesitation over inerrancy is due to their honest
judgment and not to any weakness of their evangelical convictions."[43]

Like Pinnock, and for that matter Schaeffer and Lindsell, Daniel
Fuller holds with the Lausanne Covenant that the Bible is "without
error in all that it affirms." But Fuller, a professor of hermeneutics

at Fuller Theological Seminary, would understand Scripture's inerrancy in a still different sense. Rather than take as his criterion for
judgment either the principle of "factual" accuracy or the principle
of the author's immediate intention, Fuller proposes that inerrancy
must be posited only in terms of the Bible's "overall purpose," i. e.,
in terms of the intention of God who inspired it. This purpose is for
Fuller stated clearly in 2 Timothy 3:15; it is to make us "wise unto
salvation."[44]

Although the *whole* Bible is revelational and thus inerrant in
fulfilling its intention (something Fuller repeatedly affirms in spite of
criticism by some like Lindsell),[45] those things in Scripture which are
incidentally related to the completion of this revelational intention
can be labeled "non-revelatory" matters. Furthermore, our inductive
study shows that some of these incidental "non-revelatory" statements in Scripture related to "geology, meteorology, cosmology, bot-
any, astronomy, geography, etc." are quite probably fallible (e. g.,
Stephen's speech relating Abraham's chronology in Acts 7:1–4, or
Jesus' allusion to the mustard seed as the smallest seed in Matt.
13:32).[46] But this should not concern us, for the intention and purpose
of the Biblical writers is to set forth revelational truths alone:

> being verbally inspired, the Biblical writers were also super-
> naturally enabled by God to understand the best way to take
> certain non-revelational, cultural matters, and without chang-
> ing them, use them to enhance the communication of revela-
> tional truths to the original hearers or readers.[47]

To use more accurate, but as yet unknown, judgments in non-
revelatory matters would, in fact, have distracted the hearers' attention away from the intended revelational point.

Fuller is willing to pursue his grammatical-historical methodology
relentlessly. Thus, while "inerrancy" concerning revelatory matters is
a necessary induction based on a critical study of 2 Timothy 3:15, it
is only a "highly probable" deduction when applied to all of Scripture.
If error could somehow be shown in matters that are said to be
revelatory (those incapable of "being checked out by human investigation") or in matters which are non-revelatory but serve as the basis
for revelation (those matters germane to the "whole counsel of God"
where "historical control is possible"), then the entire Bible would

become questionable, Fuller believes. Humbly, Fuller concludes with these words, "I sincerely hope that as I continue my historical-grammatical exegesis of Scripture, I shall find no error in its teachings."[48]

Fuller's inductive historicist perspective thus undercuts his sure knowledge of Scripture's authority. Historical research, rather than the Holy Spirit, is said to bring certainty to one's faith in Scripture as authoritative. The Spirit acts, but only to help the Christian be docile before the text and to submit to the results of its grammatical-historical investigation in faith. "Inerrancy" remains at best an ongoing hope, and "authority," a pious belief.

4. Complete Infallibility

Similar to Pinnock, but declining to use the word "inerrancy" because of its modern connotations, is David Hubbard. As president of Fuller Seminary, Hubbard has been called on repeatedly to justify the change which he presided over in his seminary's Statement of Faith. In the seminary's original statement, adopted in 1950, the section pertaining to Scripture read as follows:

> The books which form the canon of the Old and New Testaments as originally given are plenarily inspired and free from all error in the whole and in the part. These books constitute the written Word of God, the only infallible rule of faith and practice.[49]

In Fuller's revised statement which was announced in 1970, this section was modified to read:

> Scripture is an essential part and trustworthy record of this divine self-disclosure. All the books of the Old and New Testaments, given by divine inspiration, are the written Word of God, the only infallible rule of faith and practice. They are to be interpreted according to their context and purpose and in reverent obedience to the Lord who speaks through them in living power.[50]

What has been deleted from the first statement is the phrase "free from error in the whole and in the part." What has been included is the recognition of the need for reverent, yet critical, interpretation.

For Hubbard, the inspiration, infallibility, and authority of Scripture are givens. Here the evangelical consensus is strong and must be maintained. Scripture "must stand as teacher and judge of all that we think and do. It both inspires and corrects our doctrine and our conduct."[51] One's view of Scripture is pivotal, and submission to its full authority is basic to the evangelical faith.

While the term "inerrancy" served to underscore, in past generations, "the fact that Scripture is indeed God's trustworthy Word in all it affirms," it has provided a mixed legacy according to Hubbard. For the term "inerrancy," if left undefined, misleads in at least five ways. First, "it implies a precision alien to the minds of the Bible writers and their own use of Scriptures." Second, it causes the church's attention to be directed from the Bible's chief purpose (its message of salvation) to secondary matters. Third, it encourages superficial scholarship rather than serious Biblical wrestling for fear that one proven "error" will call all of one's faith in doubt. Fourth, as used in most evangelical discussion, the term is a philosophical judgment controlled by categories alien to Scripture; it is a slogan based on "how God ought to have inspired the Word" which has been substituted for careful patient analysis of what the Bible does teach about itself. Last, and paradoxically, the word "inerrancy" undermines its apologetic intent by reflecting a defensiveness toward Scripture that is out of keeping with the gospel's own boldly proclaimed confidence.[52] For these reasons, Hubbard has become increasingly uncomfortable with the use of the term "inerrancy" to describe his basic commitment to Scripture's infallibility, though he has no basic argument with those like Pinnock who use the term as qualified and understood Biblically.

"Errancy" is not an option for Hubbard. The Bible's infallibility and truthfulness are taken as a matter of faith, confirmed by the Holy Spirit and witnessed to by scholarly investigation. The option to "inerrancy" for Hubbard is not "errancy," but the "total infallibility" of the Bible in matters pertaining to its intention. He refrains from judgment on other matters (except perhaps to remark on Scripture's remarkable accuracy). Instead of emphasizing Scripture's "inerrancy," thinks Hubbard, those wishing to strengthen the evangelicals' commitment to Scripture's authority should stress the importance of interpretation. A positive Biblical scholarship can do much toward

learning the context, literary genre, and purpose of each portion of
God's Word. Hubbard is, in this way, arguing for an inductive methodology as the proper means of enfleshing and defining one's commitment to Scripture's infallibility. He states:

> Dealing with the Bible is not unlike the basic rule of golf:
> we must play the ball where it lies. We must not let either
> friends or enemies of the faith force us to use strategies of
> defense or interpretation that do not reckon with the reality of
> the Bible itself.[53]

As God's Word, the Bible is authoritative for the Christian, the final
and absolute norm over all Christian thought, including our understanding of its own infallibility.

An interesting permutation of Fuller Seminary's "complete infallibility" position which Hubbard defends is that of his colleague Paul
King Jewett. Jewett takes the full authority and infallibility of Scripture with utmost seriousness. In his recent book in which he argues
the role of women, he claims that he has tried to appeal "only to
Scripture, not to physiology, psychology, or sociology" as many others do.[54] As Jewett attempts to let Scripture mold his thought, however, he finds within the writings of St. Paul inconsistencies relating
to the role and place of women in the church and home. He does not
find an underlying unity among the various parts of Scripture (a basic
Reformation principle of interpretation), but believes that Paul's writings contain contradictions concerning women. On the one hand,
Paul argues for women's submission and subordination to men (1 Cor.
11; 14; 1 Tim. 2; Eph. 5); on the other, he recognizes the egalitarian
thrust of redemption (Gal. 3:28), bringing into effect a new creation
(cf. Gen. 1:26–27). Wishing to let Scripture remain totally authoritative and infallible in faith and life, Jewett appeals to a second Reformation principle of interpretation—namely, that Scripture must be
understood in light of other Scripture. As Jewett seeks to let Scripture
interpret itself, he believes he must allow it to correct its own "errors,"
revealing its higher truth in the process. Paul "the rabbi" must be
countered by Paul "the Christian"; Scripture as human (reflecting the

historical limitations of its authors' insight) must be contrasted with Scripture as divine.[55]

Such is Jewett's methodology in his recent book *Man as Male and Female.* His discussion will be looked at in some length in the next chapter. Suffice it to say here that Jewett provides strong evidence, by example, of the need to conjoin a notion of Biblical infallibility with an adequate method of interpretation. Although Jewett chaired the committee which formulated Fuller's revised Statement of Faith and recognized the need to move the discussion concerning Biblical authority from the issue of inerrancy to that of interpretation, the argument in his book is inadequate at this very point. At the moment when new insight as to the context and purpose of the supposed "chauvinist" passages in Paul is surfacing, Jewett has surprisingly abandoned his efforts to find consistency in Paul's writing. Instead, he has used the concept of "progressive revelation" to allow for the "historical limitation of . . . [Paul's] Christian insight." Paul, according to Jewett, was in error.

Lindsell claims that Jewett has openly denied by his book the Fuller Statement of Faith which declares the Bible to be "the infallible rule of faith and practice."[56] A faculty and trustee committee at Fuller which investigated the theological implications of *Man as Male and Female* found Lindsell's charge unwarranted, recognizing Jewett's sincere desire to subscribe fully to the seminary's Statement of Faith. Jewett believes his methods and conclusions are "not only consistent with, but required by, a wholehearted commitment to the infallibility of Scripture, rightly interpreted."[57] But the committee also expressed publicly their strong "regret" that "Dr. Jewett has not been more careful to make clear how he maintained the authority and integrity of all the Scriptures as they pertain to the topic discussed in his book."[58] With the publication of Jewett's book the question of "error" is seen to be a pertinent topic for discussion concerning Biblical authority, even among those holding to a position of "complete infallibility." But the issue of "error" (and thus of "inerrancy") follows, rather than precedes, the more primary issue of interpretation.

Questions to Be Answered

The above description of the range of evangelical opinion relating to a doctrine of inspiration has raised a number of questions. It has also pointed in helpful directions. From the discussion of inspiration it appears that the real issue is not that of effective apologetics, but one of theological *interpretation*. How do we rightly judge the implications of Scripture's inspiration? A whole series of questions relating to terminology, method, theological ordering, authorial intention, and cultural accommodation must be raised as central to this task of interpretation.

1. Proper Terminology: Inerrant or Infallible?

Little except terminology separates the mediating positions of Hubbard and Pinnock. Each recognizes the reasons behind the other's terminology. Each recognizes the need for all terms to be qualified hermeneutically. Each rejects the hermeneutical extremes that refuse to admit the role of higher criticism on the one hand or that use hermeneutical procedures to call into question Scripture's integrity and complete authority on the other.

"Inerrant" and "infallible" are both strong adjectives describing Scripture's total authority and trustworthiness. But though the words are often considered synonymous in English usage, there are important nuances theologically that should not be overlooked. "Inerrant" implies that the theological text under consideration is without mistake in all that it affirms. "Infallible" suggests that the text is incapable of teaching deception. One emphasizes precision and accuracy; the other, trustworthiness. The one stresses freedom from error; the other emphasizes indefectible authority. The one stresses the original purity of the text; the other, its continuing, life-giving power. "Inerrant" easily bogs down in minor detail; "infallible" seeks to validate the central truths of the gospel. "Inerrant," when qualified hermeneutically, seems to die the death of a thousand qualifications. "Infallible," on the other hand, invites all interpretive procedures which allow for a full reading of the author's intention in his communication, understood in the historical situation from which and to which he speaks. The one leads the evangelical toward a defensive apologetic; the other, to a more confident proclamation.

Although Biblical "infallibility" thus seems the better of the two options, as even Pinnock's most recent statements imply, the term is not without its problems within and outside the evangelical community.[59] Given the history of controversy over inspiration, to say that Scripture is "infallible" seems to many evangelicals a watered-down statement, one sidestepping Biblical truth. Moreover, to the larger Christian community, the term's double negative no longer suggests the positive trust in the dynamic authority of Scripture's gospel witness which has been evangelicalism's hallmark.

Perhaps the compromise wording of the Lausanne Covenant offers a third alternative to the current impasse over terminology. Rather than use either "inerrant" or "infallible," it opted to express the nature of Scripture as inspired by speaking of its "truthfulness." Inter-Varsity Christian Fellowship has also shown wisdom in this matter, choosing in its public affirmation of faith to confess "the entire trustworthiness" of the Bible. In this manner the semantic debate has been sidestepped, the defensive posture of a double negative transformed, and a forceful witness to the nature of Scripture communicated. Undoubtedly terms like "truthful" and "trustworthy" have the same potential for theological game-playing as has characterized the dispute over "inerrancy" and "infallibility." But such terms do at present discourage sloganeering, inviting instead the use of helpful qualifying phrases in order to highlight nuances of meaning that the single terms leave ambiguous.

2. Proper Methodology: Inductive or Deductive?

As evangelicals have discussed the doctrine of inspiration, two different approaches have been used. Inerrantists have most often opted for a process of *deduction.* Because God is perfect and the Bible is God's Word, the Bible, it is claimed, must be perfect. Or again, because God cannot "lie" and because the Bible is "God-breathed" (inspired), it is concluded that the Bible must be inerrant. Infallibilists have almost exclusively used a process of *induction.* Because the Bible is a human document, its data can be investigated and formulated into a structure of truth. Accepting Scripture's claim to being inspired, the interpreter will investigate the remaining phenomena of Scripture in order to understand how this claim of inspiration is enfleshed.

Both a deductive and an inductive approach have their weaknesses. The danger of fundamentalism (i. e., theology having no real connection with the historical data) on the one hand, is met by the danger of humanism (i. e., theology having no transcendent norm) on the other. Observers like Lindsell seem to have little feeling for the phenomena of Scripture, i. e., the variety of words and statements found in the text itself. Those like Beegle, on the other hand, seem to have little appreciation for the doctrine of Scripture, i. e., the importance of maintaining its message to be authoritative and inspired. A deductive methodology allows for a tidier package, but only by stuffing all the loose ends into its box; an inductive approach appears to be more faithful to the text, but it can also easily turn God's-Word-as-human-words into merely human words.

Although a deductive approach more easily allows one to maintain the unity of Scripture by suspending judgment concerning supposed difficulties in the text, it has several problems which have caused the majority of evangelicals to opt for an inductive methodology. To begin, a deduction inhibits an honest critical testing of the data. Instead of listening openly to the words of Scripture, a norm is set up concerning their meaning, and then the evidence is made to conform to it. Even more damaging, if the data cannot be brought into conformity with the norm of "inerrancy," then the whole notion of inspiration is undermined and threatened. To avoid such a possibility, deductivists have often set up unfalsifiable criteria for judging an error to be error (e. g., must be in the nonexistent autograph; must be proved beyond doubt). The reader is in this way always left with a conceivable (even if unlikely) option.

Perhaps the greatest weakness in the deductive approach is the original syllogism on which it is based: one that moves from "God cannot lie," through "Scripture is God's Word," to "Scripture is inerrant." Although the major and minor premises are easily defended as Biblical, the conclusion is unsupportable either in terms of compelling logic or direct Biblical support. The original premise declares that God is free from all deception, deceit, and falsehood. This is a far different claim from the one that all incorrectness (even unintended and incidental) has been removed from God's-Word-as-human-words, i. e., that Scripture is inerrant. Lying is something different from making a statement that has a technical inaccuracy.

It is for this reason that those using the term "infallible," as well as inerrantists like Clark Pinnock and Daniel Fuller, have opted for an inductive method of interpretation. Surely, the seminal article in evangelical circles concerning an inductive approach is Everett Harrison's "The Phenomena of Scripture" which has been widely quoted. Appearing in 1958 in *Revelation and the Bible,* edited by Carl Henry, Harrison's essay set forth the following thesis:

> No view of Scripture can indefinitely be sustained if it runs counter to the facts. That the Bible claims inspiration is patent. The problem is to define the nature of that inspiration in the light of the phenomena contained therein.[60]

In the article, Harrison discusses such "difficulties" in the text as problems with chronologies, differences in numbers, non-parallel accounts in the Gospels, the differences between John and the synoptics, and presumed error in the sources quoted (e. g., Acts 7:4). He argues, "We may have our own ideas as to how God should have inspired the Word, but it is more profitable to learn, if we can, how he has actually inspired it." Harrison still believes that inerrancy "is a natural corollary of full inspiration," but he realizes that the term must be understood according to the full phenomena of the text.[61] Harrison accepts Scripture's claim that it is inspired. As such he accepts the Bible as trustworthy (here is his meaning of "inerrancy") and authoritative. But he believes a method of induction is necessary in order to understand the full nature of Scripture's trustworthiness as inspired. Non-Biblical criteria for inerrancy must not be applied.

3. Proper Ordering: Primary or Secondary?

Detailed inerrantists claim that "inerrancy" is the crucial doctrine of evangelical Christianity. If Christians make a concession at this point, they will lack an adequate foundation for their beliefs. According to Lindsell, for example, given a retreat from inerrancy, there is an almost inevitable decline in Christian zeal and evangelism, a tendency toward spiritual sloth, and a high likelihood of apostasy.[62] The issue of theological priority hinges partly on the question of terminology (did Jesus really hold to "inerrancy"?; see question 1 above:

"Proper Terminology: Inerrant or Infallible?"); partly it concerns method (can one deduce that "false in one implies false in all"?; see question 2: "Proper Methodology: Inductive or Deductive?"); but primarily it is a matter of theological interpretation. Here, modern-day inerrantists can learn from one of their patriarchs, B. B. Warfield. Commenting on his understanding of the nature of inspiration, he wrote:

> Let it not be said that thus we found the whole Christian system upon the doctrine of plenary inspiration. We found the whole Christian system on the doctrine of plenary inspiration as little as we found it upon the doctrine of angelic existences. Were there no such thing as inspiration, Christianity would be true, and all its essential doctrines would be credibly witnessed to us in the generally trustworthy reports of the teaching of our Lord and of His authoritative agents in founding the Church, preserved in the writings of the apostles and their first followers . . . . Inspiration is not the most fundamental of Christian doctrines.[63]

Moreover, even if inspiration were the most fundamental of Christian doctrines, inerrancy would still be a derivative concern. Inspiration is the basis of inerrancy, not vice versa. To turn a particular view of inspiration, i. e., inerrancy, into the "essence" of Christianity is to confuse one's priorities concerning the Christian faith.[64] While maintaining the doctrine of *sola scriptura,* evangelicals must resist any attempt to elevate one inference from its subsidiary doctrine of inspiration to a position of ascendancy over *solus Christus, sola gratia, sola fide,* and *sola scriptura* itself.

Though the argument for the priority of inerrancy is most often couched in apologetic terms, the real focus of the issue is, I suspect, epistemological. The question is this: do we need *convincing objective reasons* prior to our faith, or can we rely on the Holy Spirit's witness to Christ heard through the Biblical evidence? No longer admitting that the witness of the Holy Spirit in and through the Word is sufficient, certain evangelicals have attempted to develop rationalistic supports for their faith. One can map out the scenario as follows:

> a.   Some evangelicals subordinate the Holy Spirit's inner witness as a basis for Scripture's self-validating authority.

b.   Wanting, nevertheless, to maintain Scripture as God's Word, they overwhelm Scripture's humanity by its divinity.

c.   Lacking a sure word from the Spirit, they must look for rationalistic supports for their faith in Scripture.

d.   They find this in the notion of inerrancy.

e.   But this causes a reversal of the relationship of inerrancy and inspiration,

f.   and a transformation of Scripture into a textbook of dogmatic truth.

g.   Moreover, the credibility of Christianity now comes to hinge on the defense of inerrancy.

Here is the irony: we try to secure the Bible's authority by claiming that it is inerrant; but to show that it is inerrant we apply "a norm external to the Bible to which the Bible must conform if it is to be regarded as true"; and discover, finally, that by this norm we are compelled to admit that "the truth of the Bible can only be established as highly *probable.* "[65] The Reformers took a different approach. Calvin, for example, believed Scripture to be self-evidencing and self-validating. "It comes with its own credentials and hence is not to be accredited by our critical judgment of external evidence."[66] How are these credentials heard? Calvin's answer is clear: the inner, objective witness of the Holy Spirit to the Word.[67] Here is the God-given certainty that faith needs.

4. The Author's Intention: Useful or Extraneous?

Evangelicals have increasingly recognized the necessity of describing Scripture's authority and trustworthiness in terms of its intention. As the Lausanne Covenant asserts, the Bible is "without error in all that it *affirms.* " Although detailed inerrantists like John Montgomery and Harold Lindsell resist referring to the writer's intentions as a criterion for Biblical judgment, sensing, rightly, that its adoption undermines their position, they nevertheless use such a standard on occasion (see Lindsell's discussion of differences in Biblical numbers [Num. 25:9; 1 Cor. 10:8], the mustard seed problem [Matt. 13:31–32], and the difficulty concerning Pekah's reign [2 Kings 15:27]).[68] Evangelicals are coming to understand that a careful assessment of the author's intention is necessary if they are "to break the empiricist tyranny" of certain evangelicals who would impose their "own narrow view of factuality" on the larger evangelical community, not letting the reader "see the Bible as it really is, and in its own terms."[69]

While agreeing on the need to take the author's intention seriously, evangelicals are divided on what constitutes that intention and what is its significance. Pinnock's concept of intention, for example, allows that "the Bible *contains* errors but *teaches* none."[70] That is, there are "errors" in the text, but they are incidental to what the author was trying to communicate to the reader. Fuller finds in II Timothy 3:15 (to make "wise unto salvation," KJV) the overall intent of Scripture and then uses this to distinguish between revelatory and non-revelatory matters in the text. Jewett, to give yet a third example, argues that the basic intention of Paul concerning the role of women is revealed in Galatians 3:28, and that this must be used in judging inadequate the intention of some of Paul's other statements concerning women ("the problem with the concept of female subordination is that it *breaks the analogy of faith*").[71]

What can be said? While the previous three questions were more easily answered, no solution exists within evangelicalism at present concerning the proper use or significance of the author's intention for an adequate interpretive framework. All three examples cited have their weaknesses. It is surely misleading to say with Pinnock that the Bible "*contains* errors but *teaches* none." If an approximation is given numerically, or if freedom with the original sources is an agreed-upon procedure, are we really to label these "errors"? One does not call poetry, or historical novels, or mythology erroneous, merely because they follow other norms of precision than scientific treatise. In an analogous way, Scripture's statements must be judged according to their intended literary genre and context.

Fuller's understanding seems to blur the distinction between the intention of the Bible as a whole and the intention of a particular Biblical text. While Scripture's overall intention is, indeed, to make us "wise unto salvation," this is not the aim of each individual passage, at least not in the same way. The main intent of 1 Corinthians 11 is to deal with order in the church; of Genesis 5, to provide a chronology for the descendants of Adam; and of Psalm 8, to sing of the glory of God as Creator. Rather than sift the Scripture according to the general principle of its applicability to salvation, wouldn't it be better to inquire of each text what was its intended message? Only in this way can God's multifaceted revelation be heard on its own terms without narrowing it to traditional salvation-categories.

Jewett's alternative raises a related problem. He would take a specific example of Scripture's truth of salvation—the equality of male and female in Christ—and use it to dismiss the intent of other Biblical texts as sub-Christian. In this way, Scripture is being interpreted and judged according to other Scripture, in a way that undermines the authority and trustworthiness of all the Scriptures in their parts. Instead of such a self-defeating hermeneutic, it would seem better to hold to the unity of Scripture in its parts and whole, even while continuing to seek the individual author's intention and historical context for those clues that would allow us to maintain Scripture's integrity. Unintentionally, Jewett has used the notion of intention to undercut *sola scriptura,* the very principle he seeks to affirm.

It is, of course, easier to criticize other attempts than to propose a constructive alternative. But the above comments should indicate the direction which further refinements on the notion of intention must take. What is unintended cannot be judged as erroneous. What is intended must be judged according to each particular passage. And the intent of individual texts must be investigated from a posture that assumes the overall trustworthiness of the text.

5. Historical Accommodation?

In seeking to maintain a high view of inspiration, evangelicals have wrestled with the fact that God's revelation was stated in terms of the language, logic, and location of the people to whom it was originally written. Though Scripture is the "truth" of God, it is truth historically accommodated to the human mind and understanding. While this fact is widely recognized, it is given a variety of interpretations within the evangelical community, many of which prove inadequate on further reflection.

Conservatives such as Lindsell have resisted all attempts to use "accommodation" as a justification for formal error in the text. They have challenged the notion that the Biblical writers were men of their times in respect to history, cosmology, and physics, who wrote what they believed to be true but what is now known to be false. Any error in the text, even on a point incidental to the author's intention, is considered to undermine radically Scripture's usefulness. Even if the Biblical writers personally held to that which we know to be erroneous, the Holy Spirit kept them from including those things in Scripture. For example, Lindsell states: "They may have believed that the sun revolves around the earth, but they did not teach this in Scripture."[72] For Lindsell, accommodation has to do with the form of revelation, but it in no way impinges on the content of Scripture.

Daniel Fuller believes that in non-revelatory matters, there is "error" in the Biblical text which was included deliberately by the authors in order to communicate effectively with their readers. He posits, for example, that Jesus in his omniscience knew that there were smaller seeds than the mustard seed, but nevertheless used "this facet of the culture of the people to whom he was speaking as a vehicle for conveying the cargo of revelational truth."[73] Had Jesus been more scientifically accurate, he would have merely confused his audience. Fuller quotes Calvin approvingly at this point. Referring to the use in the book of Hebrews of a faulty Septuagintal translation in order to make a point (Heb. 11:21: *mittah* [bed] has been confused with *matteh* [staff], cf. Gen. 47:31), Calvin writes: "The Apostle hesitated not to apply to his purpose what was commonly received . . . . And we know that the Apostles were not so scrupulous in this respect, as not to accommodate themselves to the unlearned."[74]

Paul Jewett maintains still a third notion of accommodation. He believes Paul's statements regarding female subordination can best be understood by recognizing "the human as well as the divine quality of Scripture." Paul was as an apostle still a partial captive to his rabbinic past. Thus, although he proclaimed a major theological "breakthrough" when he wrote that in Christ there is neither male nor female, Paul failed to understand the social implications of this truth and remained chauvinistic in some of his practical advice to the churches. His writing reflects "the historical limitations of his Christian insight."[75] Paul's accommodation to his times, in other words, causes him occasionally to come short of God's revealed intent for humanity.

With Lindsell, Scripture is culturally independent; with Fuller, it is culturally conditioned; with Jewett, culturally limited. I would suggest that all three formulations are deficient and work to undercut an adequate notion of inspiration. Concerning Lindsell's position, careful critical study of the text reveals that accommodation has to do with content as well as form (e.g., Heb. 11:21 and Gen. 47:31). Concerning Fuller's claims, it is highly conjectural to posit that all accommodation in Scripture is deliberate. Moreover, it is not clear that "error" in non-revelatory material is *necessary* in order to communicate effectively. Jewett has mistakenly contrasted the human with the divine (evangelicals have consistently held the whole of Scripture to be at one and the same time human *and* divine), rather than contrasting the divine principles with their more limited cultural application. Concerning female subordination, accommodation does not have to do with Paul's historical limitation of knowledge, but his historical focus in the application of the knowledge he possesses.

Rather than any of the above models, I would suggest that evangelicals might better look at the notion of accommodation in terms of Scripture's cultural-directedness. Jesus himself provides us our hermeneutical key in his discussion with the Pharisees concerning the Mosaic law on divorce (Mark 10:3–5). Citing Genesis 1 and 2 which speak of marriage's indissolubility, Jesus sees this as God's primary will for married couples. Jesus, then, interprets Moses' allowance for divorce in Deuteronomy 24:1, 3 as being on account of the people's "hardness of heart." The Deuteronomic commandment, in other words, is God's inspired revelation to his people—it is trustworthy and authoritative—but it must be understood both in terms of the historical realities of life in ancient Israel (the people's sin) and in terms of God's wider revelation in the whole of Scripture. Interpreted in this light, the Mosaic text witnesses to a divine accommodation. It is culturally directed and must be understood as such, though this does not allow us to dismiss it as a faulty socialization—a mere assumption of the author. No, the Mosaic text is at one and the same time God's Word and human words—divinely inspired and culturally directed. As such, it remains fully inspired and authoritative.

Conclusion

On each of the questions discussed above, matters of theological interpretation prove basic. Moreover, the hermeneutical keys for constructing adequate theological responses come from all three of the sources of theological insight—contemporary sensitivity, investigation into the tradition, and reevaluation of the Biblical texts. The issue of terminology hinges on a proper reading of current sensibilities in evangelical circles. The issue of theological priority is illumined by a consideration of traditional formulations such as those of Warfield. The question of historical accommodation is addressed by an exegetical appeal to the tenth chapter of Mark. Thus, to deal with issues involving inspiration is more than to make an apologetic appeal to the character of Scripture's autographs which we no longer possess. It is, instead, to take seriously the issue of theological interpretation. If discussion of inspiration is to prove fruitful in evangelical circles, it must move from dogmatic statement to matters of concrete theological judgment.

Such an agenda will no doubt prove difficult, for the link in evangelical circles between inspiration and apologetics is a strong one. Inspiration has become, for many, the cornerstone for a defense of the faith. With the focus on "inerrancy," however, much of the balance and vitality within the evangelical theological enterprise is being lost. The results are proving serious. The task of confronting the non-evangelical world over the issue of Biblical authority is being undercut by the desire to challenge fellow evangelicals' notions of inspiration. What is distinctively evangelical needs again to be forcefully presented to the wider Christian community. Again, the important task of adjudicating differences of opinion on other theological issues within the evangelical community is being largely preempted (recent meetings of the Evangelical Theological Society, for example, have often become one-topic convocations). Evangelicals need to take more seriously the significant differences that exist concerning a wide range of theological issues. Evangelicals need also to reaffirm the large area of theological common ground which is now being overlooked in the internecine debate over inspiration. The very strength of evangelical commonality is being unnecessarily weakened. Finally, evangelicals face the real danger of bolstering an un-Biblical theology of inspiration either under the cloak of faithful orthodoxy on the one hand, or of critical scholarship on the other. With the focus of discussion concerning inspiration being on apologetics rather than on constructive theology, such excesses and destructive tendencies seem inevitable.

The real issue concerning a doctrine of inspiration centers on complex matters of interpretation—issues which I have attempted to speak to in the discussion above. It is to these matters that the evangelical church must turn, if their present impasse is to be overcome and consensus gained.

III

The Role of Women in the Church and Family: The Issue of Biblical Hermeneutics

It is almost impossible for the interested individual to keep abreast of the burgeoning discussion among evangelicals on women's place in the church and Christian family. Stirred by the steady stream of feminist literature which has caused a revolution in Western society, and prodded by the more liberal wing of the church which opened up the discussion on the ordination of women twenty or more years ago, contemporary evangelicals have become increasingly interested in reevaluating the role of women.*

As the discussion has proceeded among evanglicals, sides have been drawn.[5] One faction is represented by supporters of the Evangelical Women's Caucus like Nancy Hardesty, Lucille Sider Dayton, and Virginia Mollenkott. The other, by such otherwise disparate individu-

---

*Books such as Marabel Morgan's *The Total Woman*, Virginia Mollenkott's *Women, Men, and the Bible*, Helen Andelin's *Fascinating Womanhood*, Don Williams's *The Apostle Paul and Women in the Church*, Larry Christenson's *The Christian Family*, Gladys Hunt's *Ms. Means Myself*, Paul Jewett's *Man as Male and Female*, Letha Scanzoni's and Nancy Hardesty's *All We're Meant to Be*, Elisabeth Elliot's *Let Me Be a Woman*, and George W. Knight's *The New Testament Teaching on the Role Relationship of Men and Women* have taken varying positions and have been widely read and debated in evangelical circles.[1] Bill Gothard, through his Institute in Basic Youth Conflicts, has offered teaching on the subject of women's rightful place to thousands, as have Francis Schaeffer, Howard Hendricks, and Tim LaHaye. Evangelical periodicals such as *The Other Side* (July-August 1973), *Right On* (September 1975), *Post American* (August-September 1974), *Theology, News and Notes* (June 1975), and *The Wittenburg Door* (August-September 1975) have devoted whole issues to the topic of women.[2] Other journals like *Christianity Today, Moody Monthly, Logos, The Reformed Journal, Eternity, Vanguard,* and *Sojourners* have published repeated articles on the issue.[3] *Daughters of Sarah* has come into being to provide for evangelical women who believe Christianity and feminism are inseparable.[4]

als as George Knight, Elisabeth Elliot, and Larry Christenson. The one side argues that a Christian woman in today's society should be ordained to ministry if she possesses the gifts and has the training. It also holds that wives should join their husbands in egalitarian relationships characterized by *mutual* love and submission. The other side argues that a female in today's "liberated" society is still a "woman" and as such should fit into God's ordained and orderly creation, fulfilling her role of submission and dependence in church and family without impatience on the one hand or servitude on the other.

From the earliest days of the current discussion, it has been recognized that the question regarding the role of women within the congregation and the family is largely a matter of Biblical interpretation. Krister Stendahl gave voice to this in his important essay *The Bible and the Role of Women: A Case Study in Hermeneutics* written in 1958.[6] Donald Dayton expressed a similar position in his article in the *Post American:* "the real question—at least for most Christians [is]: Which of these views (the hierarchical or the egalitarian—or perhaps a synthesis of the two) has the clearer grounding in scripture?"[7]

Use of the Bible as the source of authority in the debate has brought mixed approaches and results. Feminists have tended to emphasize the broader affirmations of the gospel which stress oneness in Christ. Traditionalists have usually centered on specific passages of advice in Scripture such as Ephesians 5:22 ("Wives, be subject to your husbands") and 1 Timothy 2:12 ("I permit no woman to teach or to have authority over men; she is to keep silent"). Feminists have turned first to the Gospels and Acts; traditionalists to the epistles. Given such differences in approach, it is not surprising that in regard to the interpretation of specific Biblical texts, contradictory opinions have arisen at almost every conceivable place. Does man's "headship" as referred to by Paul relate to his rank in "authority" or to his role as "provider" and "source"? Is Paul's use of Genesis in his discussion of woman's place illustrative or foundational? Is the curse in Genesis 3:16 descriptive or prescriptive?* Both sides have grounded their

---

*Such questioning seems endless once begun. Is the Biblical picture normative (with its male predominance), or are there deeper principles implicit in the texture of the Biblical fabric which make male authority a cultural, and thus relative, affair? Is the

positions in Scripture, but because of differing understandings of the text, they have reached opposite conclusions.

The issue of women's place in the church and family provides us another illustration of the general problem facing the evangelical church in America today. That is, how can evangelicals maintain their theoretical paradigm of Biblical authority while subscribing to contradictory positions on a variety of significant theological issues? What is at stake in the discussion of women is more than the surface issue, important as that is. What is being challenged by the continuing debate is the nature and efficacy of Biblical authority itself.

If evangelicals are to move beyond their current impasse, a clarification concerning their method of understanding Scripture must be made. For behind the apparent differences in approach and opinion regarding the women's issue are opposing principles for interpreting Scripture—i. e., different hermeneutics. Here is the real issue facing evangelical theology as it seeks to answer the women's question.

In order that readers can appreciate this fact, I will do three things in this chapter. First, I will present further descriptions of the contrasting positions—the egalitarian and the traditionalist. In doing this, I will state as fairly as possible composite views of the arguments of major representatives of each approach. With this as background, I will then discuss certain assumptions in Biblical interpretation cur-

---

first-century life-style prepared or happenstance as it correlates with revelation, or perhaps some of each? Is it significant that Jesus was a male and appointed only male disciples? What is the significance of Jesus' "revolutionary" attitude and actions toward women? Does "subordination" imply inferiority? Is the order of creation normative or has it been superseded by the fact of redemption? Can the Trinity serve as a model of submissiveness within a context of equality? Does the fact that woman was made for man imply a hierarchy? Is the use of the masculine gender for God still significant for us today? Was the advice by Paul concerning women meant to be applied universally or was it a response to a localized need? Is it important that women in the Old Testament were prophets, but never priests? What is the meaning of words like *authentein* (1 Tim. 2:12) and *exousia* (1 Cor. 11:10)?

Are the arguments Paul uses in 1 Corinthians 11 meant to pertain to all men and women or only to the husband-wife relationship? Does Galatians 3:28 refer to a woman's "spiritual privilege" of being saved, or does it refer to her position and activity in the church and Christian family as well? Are women more easily led astray than men (1 Pet. 3:7)? Does the fact that man was created first, according to Genesis, matter? When Paul speaks about women, is he referring to all women or only to wives (remembering that women in those days married young)? Do all the details of Paul's advice to women apply equally today? If not, how do you decide what is normative? Such questions are basic to understanding a Biblical position regarding women in the church and family and are answered variously by each side in the debate.

rently surfacing in evangelical circles. Finally, I will offer suggestions for an adequate hermeneutic together with indications of its helpfulness in the discussion of women's role in the church and family. The issue of women's rightful role can prove instructive for the theological task of the church more generally, particularly as it focuses the issue of Biblical authority at the point of an adequate method of Biblical interpretation.

An Egalitarian Position

What is the nature of woman? Genesis 1:26, 27 recounts how God made man as male and female in his image. Man and woman were to be a fellowship of equals like the fellowship within the Godhead (i. e., the Trinity) and were given joint responsibilities (Gen. 1:28). The second creation narrative (Gen. 2:18–23) reinforces this basic point, portraying woman as being from God like man, as well as one with him, i. e., flesh of his flesh. With the fall, the subordination of woman to man becomes a reality, the first example of exploitation in human relationships. Now Adam names his wife "Eve" (Gen. 3:20), and God describes her future relation with Adam as one of authority and submission (Gen. 3:16). This "curse" is not applied to all women, but is sheathed in the context of husband-wife relationships. Moreover, it is clear that in Christ there is a new creation, superseding the conditions of the fall:

> There is neither Jew nor Greek, there is neither slave nor free, there is neither male nor female; for you are all one in Christ Jesus. [Gal. 3:28]

Through faith by grace, the equality of male and female in human relationships is restored (1 Cor. 11:11–12).

This new creation was demonstrated in Jesus' life, as he broke with the existing hierarchical structuring of male-female relationships and treated women as equals (Luke 8:1–3; 10:38–42; 11:27–28; 13:10–17; 21:1–4; Mark 5:22–42; 16:9; John 8:3–11; 12:1–8). Within the church, similarly, women, like men, were early converts and the description of the first-century church suggests that women were engaged in significant ministry within it (1 Cor. 11:2–16; Rom. 16:1–16; Col. 4:15; Acts 2:17–21; 5:14; 8:12; 9:1–2, 36–42; 12:12; 16:12–15, 40; 17:4,

34; 18:2–3, 24–28; 21:9; Phil. 4:2–3; 1 Tim. 3:11; 5:1–16; 2 Tim. 1:5; Tit. 2:3). Moreover, the New Testament teaches that every Christian is to grow into maturity in Christ and to exercise fully the gifts she or he has been given. No sexual distinction is hinted at (2 Tim. 1:6–7; Rom. 12:6–8; 1 Pet. 4:10; 1 Cor. 12:4–31; Matt. 25:14–30).

Those passages in Scripture which seem to speak against this fundamental position of equality between men and women (1 Cor. 11:2–16; 14:33–35; 1 Tim. 2:8–15; Eph. 5:21–33; 1 Pet. 3:1–7) must be understood as follows:

1. Our existing translations are often biased against women (e. g., in 1 Tim. 2:11, "in silence" [KJV] should rather be translated "quietly" [NEB]) or archaic (e. g., in Gen. 2:18 a "help meet for him" [KJV] does not mean a subordinate "helpmate").

2. Although the fact that man and woman are to be partners in fellowship was largely overlooked in patriarchal Israel, there was even there a depatriarchalizing tendency (cf. Song of Solomon; Exod. 20:12 and Deut. 5:16: "Honor thy father and thy mother" [KJV]; Judg. 4—6). This is continued in the New Testament (Gal. 3:28).

3. Christians shared the cultural attitudes of the first century regarding the position of women in a manner analogous to their attitude toward slavery (cf. Eph. 5:21—6:9 where Paul expresses the reciprocity of marriage in terms acceptable to the Ephesians' cultural attitudes and the obligation of slaves and masters in a similar manner).

4. In Scripture, the understanding and application of revelation is a historical process (cf. Mark 10:3–5). We recognize this in relation to Christianity's influence on the emancipation of slaves. We must similarly apply this recognition to the issue of women's rightful role today.

5. Paul's letters are addressed to specific people with special problems which called for particular responses which were correct for that situation but must often be translated into underlying general principles if they are to be applicable to us today (e. g., 1 Cor. 14:33–40 probably refers to uneducated married women disrupting the order of worship by asking questions; 1 Tim. 2:8–15 may be a response to immature women believers teaching heresy in the church).

6. Paul's advice regarding women in the church must be correlated with his description of what women actually did in the early church (see above for references).

7. We must beware of reading twentieth-century nuances into first-century advice (e. g., "head" in 1 Cor. 11:3 is probably not meant to designate a hierarchy but to suggest woman's "source" or "origin" as portrayed in Gen. 2).

8. Those who want to interpret Scripture "literalistically" must be consistent in their approach. Yet few, if any, literalists are willing to do this, for they recognize that this is to treat Scripture anachronistically. (Cf. John 13:14; 1 Tim. 2:12; 5:23; and 1 Pet. 3:3. In these texts, Christians are commanded to wash one another's feet; women are prohibited from teaching men; wine is recommended as an aid to digestion; and women are told not to braid their hair or wear jewelry.)

A Traditionalist's Position

In discussing the role of women in marriage and worship, we must begin by looking at where the Bible speaks specifically to the issue, not just at passages with more general import. Regarding women in ordained ministry, there are three such didactic passages which apply to the situation (1 Cor. 11:2–16; 14:33b–35; 1 Tim. 2:11–15). These texts prohibit the church from allowing a woman to hold a teaching/ruling office. Moreover, the passages transcend cultural relativity for they are grounded in reasons always germane to man and woman: God's eternal order and purposes for men and women as reflected in creation, as well as the fall of Adam and Eve (1 Tim. 2:13–14; 1 Cor. 11:7–10; 14:34). In Ephesians 5:22–33 Paul argues for a hierarchical relationship within the family, basing his insight once again on the fact of a universal creation-ordering, one of headship and subjection. Peter similarly argues for the wife's submission to her husband, basing his advice on the Old Testament paradigm of Sarah. There is no hint that the hierarchical structuring of marriage is to be considered only an interim solution (1 Pet. 3:1–7).

As for those passages which suggest that women can publicly pray and prophesy (1 Cor. 11:5; Acts 2:17–21), it must be observed that these acts of worship are distinct from authoritative speaking, teaching, and ruling and are therefore to be allowed. Similarly, women may be involved in diaconal tasks and non-authoritative teaching functions outside the worship context (Rom. 16:1; Tit. 2:3–4; Acts 18:26; 1 Tim. 3:11; 5:9–10).

Using as a guide these passages which deal explicitly with the question of women's rightful place, it is possible to avoid making erroneous deductions from other passages in Scripture which deal with more general concerns related to women. Galatians 3:28 has become almost foundational to the cause of feminism, because egalitarians have not followed this principle. If they would, they would recognize that the key to understanding this verse is "in Christ." Although there is spiritual unity and equality "in Christ" (i. e., *coram Deo*), among mankind in the church and society there remains a necessary structuring of male and female relationships. This is symbolized by Paul's injunction concerning uncovered and covered heads (I Cor. 11). An analogous situation to woman's voluntary limitation of Christian freedom for the sake of order and stability is Paul's advice to refrain in some situations from eating meat (1 Cor. 8:13; cf. 9:19). Receipt of Christ's full inheritance must await the second coming. The temporal order (our life in the world) is not yet synonymous with the baptismal order (our life in Christ). Woman's interim position of subjection does not imply inferiority, however. One has only to compare it with Christ's voluntary submission to, yet equality with, God the Father.

There are other considerations worth mentioning:

1. No one in present-day evangelicalism took feminism seriously until it became a dominant theme in our secular, humanistic culture.

2. Certainly males predominate in Scripture. The exceptions only prove the rule. Furthermore, Jesus chose only men as his disciples and therefore as the leaders of his church. To argue for a Biblically based "feminism" is inconsistent with the entire posture of Scripture.

3. Culture is not happenstance, but prepared by God. Israel with its patriarchal system was peculiarly designed by God as his vehicle of divine truth. Moreover, in "the fullness of time" the gospel came. Thus, Christianity holds that Biblical patterns are significant and normative. They reflect the mystery of the divine order. To man is

confided the task of ruling; to woman the task of serving.

4. The symbolism of the relationship of God to his people (Hosea) and of Christ to his church (Eph. 5) demands a male officeholder in the church and a male authority in the home. Only in this way is divine authority, dominion, and supremacy adequately portrayed. We are not free to tamper with the Biblical imagery without losing some of the mystery.

5. The virgin Mary exemplifies the ideal woman in her voluntary submission and response to the will of God.

6. The principles of obedience, submission, and authority are clear in both the Old and New Testament. The teaching regarding a hierarchy in male and female relationships is only one aspect of a larger and necessary ordering of all reality that extends into the Godhead itself (cf. Christ's obedience and submission to the Father and the Holy Spirit's subordination to the Son). In the created order, this hierarchical structure provides each level of being its proper responsibility and privileges—archangels, angels, men, women, children, animals, etc.

Hermeneutical Assumptions Presently Surfacing

As these egalitarian and traditionalist positions have been argued, implicit hermeneutical procedures have been used by adherents in both camps. Whenever people read the Bible (or any other piece of literature for that matter), they make use of certain underlying interpretive principles—i. e., hermeneutical procedures. Often this interpretive framework remains unclarified, but it is always present. In the case of the current debate among evangelicals over woman's place in the church and marriage, however, the challenge of conflicting viewpoints has brought what otherwise might have remained implicit methods of interpretation to light. Moreover, problems within evangelical hermeneutics have become apparent in two areas: (1) the issue of "culture," and (2) the tendency toward inconsistency. Why these issues are of particular concern is that procedures of interpretation presently in use threaten to undermine the full authority of the Biblical record—a cardinal tenet of evangelicalism as we have already observed.

1. The Issue of "Culture"

In current discussions on women's place in the church and family there is the tendency among egalitarians to take a dualistic approach to Scripture, isolating the time-bound from the universal, the human from the divine, the rabbinic from the Christian. There is among the traditionalists a parallel tendency, that of spiritualizing Scripture by treating it ahistorically. Rather than viewing Scripture as being time-bound, it is now understood as timeless truth. The dualist stumbles over the Bible's humanness; the spiritualizer, over Scripture's "supernatural" nature. The former seems overcome by Scripture's time-relatedness; the latter seeks to deny this time-relatedness any real significance. Neither approaches Scripture as at one and the same time fully and completely God's-Word-as-human-words. Both seem unwilling to give themselves over to a fresh round of exacting, detailed research, for they are convinced already that God's Word or the human words are clear.

a. A Dualistic Approach

Virginia Mollenkott states concerning Paul's advice to women: "My training as a literary critic simply will not permit me to indulge in interpretations which depend on evidence which is not yet available." Those who want to deny that Paul at times considers women inferior do so in opposition to the clear evidence of certain Pauline statements. Convinced that certain Biblical texts allow only a chauvinistic interpretation, she concludes that though she respects Paul greatly for his central affirmation about humanity (Gal. 3:28), his words at other times fall away from that central vision. Something has interfered. She says, "I have called the interference a distortion caused by the human limitations of the human channel." Rather than consider that Paul's writings on women might have been culturally (mis)-interpreted for centuries, Mollenkott instead concludes that some of Paul's arguments reflect his "rabbinical training and human limitations."[8] "There are flat contradictions between some of his theological arguments and his own doctrines and behavior," she says.[9]

This position that there is a Pauline self-contradiction is also taken by Paul Jewett in his book *Man as Male and Female.* He believes that the inconsistency between Paul's arguments for female subordination

(e. g., 1 Tim. 2:8–15) and his fundamental awareness of Christian liberty (Gal. 3:28) can only be resolved by recognizing "the human as well as the divine quality of Scripture." Paul's historical limitations, particularly his rabbinical background, affect his Christian insight. For example, Jewett notes that 1 Corinthians 11:5–6 commands women to cover their heads:

> any woman who prays or prophesies with her head unveiled dishonors her head—it is the same as if her head were shaven. For if a woman will not veil herself, then she should cut off her hair; but if it is disgraceful for a woman to be shorn or shaven, let her wear a veil.

He finds it a "curious idea" without foundation in text or context that this injunction was meant only for that particular situation in Corinth where prostitutes did not wear veils or long hair. Conflating Old Testament practice (Gen. 38:15) with first-century Greek society, Jewett would have us understand that, perhaps, prostitutes were veiled. He concludes that Paul considered the custom of head-covering part of the apostolic tradition which he had previously given the Corinthians (in 1 Cor. 11:2, Paul commends the Corinthians for maintaining "the traditions even as I have delivered them to you"). "Thus," concludes Jewett, "the apostle elevates the relativities of culture to the absolutes of Christian piety."[10]

There are difficulties in Jewett's interpretation which even the summary reveals.[11] For example, the "traditions" referred to in verse 2 might better be taken as the central truths of the Christian faith given previously to the Corinthians by Paul in oral form, for verses 13 and 16 suggest that Paul did not consider his injunction concerning women one of the central tenets of the faith. Rather, it was based on current mores:

> Judge for yourselves; is it proper for a woman to pray to God with her head uncovered? . . . If any one is disposed to be contentious, we recognize no other practice, nor do the churches of God. [1 Cor. 11:13, 16]

The cultural situation in Corinth cannot be so quickly ignored. Again, reevaluations of the meaning of *kephale* (head) and *exousia* (authority) are not considered. But what is more important than any particular interpretive oversight is the underlying hermeneutical principle

Jewett's argument reflects. Jewett, like Mollenkott, would functionally discard those portions of Scripture which reflect human limitation, even while keeping them in the canon. Rather than struggle to understand the cultural background of the text and the alternate meanings suggested by recent historico-grammatical research, Jewett is content to judge the text as reflecting Paul's rabbinic conditioning and disregard it. It is as if Paul was a split-person, unable to resolve his conflicts of sexism and Christian liberty in a consistent manner.[12]

What is basic to both Mollenkott's and Jewett's positions is too facile an exegesis of key Biblical passages. They have accepted traditional interpretations rather than reevaluating the evidence in search of an underlying consistency in Paul's position.[13] *Behind this willingness to allow traditional interpretations to remain normative is the hermeneutical principle that the interpreter can separate that which is human from that which is divine in Scripture.* The Reformation principle that "Scripture interprets itself" *(sacra scriptura sui ipsius interpres)* is taken to mean that Scriptures which seem to conflict with the central affirmations of the gospel and the example of Christ himself are to be discarded, rather than in its original sense that there is a unity in Scripture as Biblical texts mutually interpret each other. This is, however, to set humanity over Scripture as the final arbiter of what is inspired and authoritative for Christian practice. Scripture is in danger of losing its normative nature.

Traditionalists, like Harold Lindsell, have been quick to challenge such an approach, for it undercuts Biblical authority.[14] But feminists as well, like Nancy Hardesty, are aware of the implications of this position and have sought alternate approaches:

> Unlike some feminists, I do *not* rest my conclusions on any supposed contradictions within the writings of Paul, or between Paul and Jesus, on any alleged "rabbinic interpretations," or on the cultural relativity of any text. I see no difficulty in harmonizing all of the Bible's teaching on this subject nor in harmonizing feminism with the teaching of Scripture. I do not disagree with any teaching of Scripture on this issue. I disagree, rather, with the distorted *interpretations* based on patriarchal social patterns and neo-platonic philosophical systems which men have used to obscure the radical message of the Gospel and to oppress women.[15]

Whether a feminist position is as consistent with Scripture as Hardesty believes is open to further discussion. But she is certainly correct in rejecting a *dualistic* hermeneutic. The principle of "consistency" demands not the dismissal of seemingly contradictory texts, but the ongoing reevaluation of traditional interpretations in search of distortion.

b. A "Spiritualizing" Approach

Egalitarians are not the only ones experiencing difficulty in understanding Scripture as time-related. Where some feminists reject what is time-bound, extrapolating "the essential, unconditioned truths by discarding what . . . [they consider] nonessential," some traditionalists make Scripture's time-relatedness similarly of no account by claiming that "revelation *is* available in a pure and unambiguous form."[16] This can only be done by minimizing the gap between the centuries; the interpreter forgets "to what extent Paul's words belong to a certain situation."[17]

Elisabeth Elliot (Leitch), for example, believes that the Biblical world view and culture, with its patriarchal system, was "peculiarly designed and chosen by God as a vehicle of heavenly truth":

> Are we to assume that if first century Semite culture had allowed it Jesus would have appointed women apostles and addressed God as Mother? Or shall we find in God's choice of the Judaic framework of reference, in Old Testament times as well as in New Testament ones, the sovereignty of God? For it was in "the fullness of time" that the Gospel came. It was the first century that is for the Christian Church normative.[18]

The first century is normative? By this is Elliot suggesting, for example, that the Abolitionist movement was un-Christian? That Europeans are correct to greet one another with kisses while Americans are guilty of acting non-Biblically? That we should begin to wash one another's feet? Such positions follow, it would seem, from taking first-century practices as normative. Moreover, if the patriarchal system in the Old Testament is understood as ordained by God to reflect his self-revelation, what of an absolute monarchy, or perhaps a theocracy, which Biblical authors similarly considered to be God-ordained? Why are sexual politics timeless while national politics are relative to time and place?

In her recent book *Let Me Be a Woman,* Elliot finds the key to woman's timeless place in marriage and worship in such specific references as "For man was not made from woman, but woman from man. Neither was man created for woman, but woman for man." (1 Cor. 11:8–9) "Some texts," Elliot allows, "are susceptible of differing interpretations, but for the life of me I can't see any ambiguities in this one."[19] Biblical commentators who have struggled with the meaning of Paul's advice in 1 Corinthians 11 must wish the situation was as clear-cut as Elliot maintains. Only by taking Paul's words out of both their immediate text and their cultural context is such a stance possible. Elliot has spiritualized Paul's words, taking only their surface meaning, making them timeless and mysterious in their full intent. She finds them to reflect "a divinely inspired principle" and are therefore "not negotiable."[20]

Thomas Howard takes a similar approach. He, too, sees the Biblical picture of male predominance as normative:

> the burden of particular aspects of the splendor of the Divine Image, including authority and primacy, has been placed upon the shoulders of the man; whereas the answering burden has been placed upon woman—the echo, or antiphon, to the man's aspect, without which his authority and primacy are solitary and sterile. This pattern . . . is implicit in the whole fabric of biblical narrative.

Exceptions to this ordering in Scripture are so embarrassingly few, Howard feels, that they only reinforce the basic fact.

> It was not just a random happenstance that Yahweh picked a patriarchal society to exhibit His Name in. *He* didn't take His cues from *them:* He prepared them, and ordered them, to exhibit, in the structure of their social and political and domestic and cultic life, the deepest mysteries of divinity and humanity.[21]

Howard looks at the overall picture in Scripture and finds a pattern in Biblical times that is meant for all times.

What lies, in part, behind Elliot's and Howard's common desire to maintain the "mystery" of God's hierarchical ordering is the ecclesiastical position they adhere to. With C. S. Lewis, whom they quote with respect on this point, they believe that women cannot be "priests," for the priest is to represent God. God, as they would have us know, consistently portrays himself to us as a male. Similarly the Bible uses the church's subjection to Christ as a symbol of marriage. Christians should not negate these symbols by allowing women to represent God's Word in the pulpit and sacrament or by proclaiming the validity of egalitarian relationships. To tamper with Christian imagery concerning God or his church is to destroy the sense of the "mystical" which Christianity should contain. "The Church of England," Lewis asserts, and analogously the American Episcopal Church which is Howard's and Elliot's chosen home, "can remain a church only if she retains this opaque element."[22] The timeless is maintained out of a desire for the mystical, the mysterious, the opaque. Such a theological and ecclesiological position has a long cultural heritage in Christian tradition, but it must not imperialize Biblical interpretation by becoming the sole authoritative stance from which the Biblical witness is read. When this happens, Scripture loses its normative position over Christian tradition.[23]

———————————

Jewett and Mollenkott arrive at their dualistic hermeneutic partly out of their cultural attachment to women's liberation. Howard and Elliot come to their "spiritualized" hermeneutic out of a need to buttress their high church liturgical commitment. But to conclude that only cultural and ecclesiological considerations determine these approaches would be untrue. G. C. Berkouwer, in his volume *Holy Scripture,* describes both the "dualist" and the "spiritualizer" and in the process suggests an additional common motivation for these faulty approaches to Scripture's cultural character. He states:

> one may not . . . devise from the beginning a "method" that guarantees the safety of the road of faith. One such method is that of deduction [the "spiritualizers"], which seeks to prove as conclusively as possible that Scripture exceeds all time-relatedness. Another is that of induction [the "dualists"], which often runs the risk of bogging down in a "canon of interpretation," applying a critical yardstick to God's Word and preventing a true listening to the Spirit's voice to the churches. It is the abiding Word of God alone that tests and

accompanies all study of Scripture; it challenges and encourages us to continue on this road, critically weighing all human words about God's Word, with the expectation and certainty shared with the church of all ages that the "jewel" of the gospel will not be lost in a new and still unknown future.[24]

It is this fear of losing the "jewel" of the gospel which helps to account for Jewett and Mollenkott becoming dualists, and Elliot and Howard becoming spiritualizers. Given society's growing recognition that men and women are equal, is the gospel to retain its power if it remains tied to a hierarchical structuring in which women are seen as subservient and dependent? Given the mystery of the gospel proclaimed in the symbolism of church and family, can Christians afford to dilute its strength in their desire to accommodate the latest cultural fad? Both dualist and spiritualizer believe they are protecting the gospel. But ironically, by undercutting Scripture's authoritative and culturally directed message, they end up by diminishing its power.

The evangelical interpreter of Scripture must approach the Biblical text critically, yet faithfully. Dualists expect an integrity *from* the text, but it must also be an integrity *of* the text. Spiritualizers expect of the text a cultural *relevance,* but they must also allow for an original cultural *relatedness.* Evangelicals must subject the text to the literary-critical fate of all writing. They must affirm that they do not know in advance what Scripture says. Instead of locking themselves in to what was formerly believed to be *the* correct interpretation of a passage, they must remain humble before Scripture as God's-Word-as-human-words. This evangelical hermeneutic does not guarantee one "the safety of the road of faith." Rather it demands faith, both in the gospel *per se* and in its authoritative organ of communication, Scripture. Faithful as they approach the Biblical record, evangelicals are confident of its reliability, clarity, and sufficiency. To recognize that Scripture is culturally directed and time-related does not call into question such a stance. Instead, it is the necessary posture for those who would stand reverently before God's-Word-as-human-words.[25]

2. The Tendency Toward Inconsistency

In addition to the improper handling of Scripture's cultural-directedness, there is a second area of hermeneutical concern in contemporary evangelical discussions of women's role in marriage and ministry. This is the marked propensity among evangelicals to be inconsistent in their handling of the Biblical sources. This inconsistency takes two major forms: (a) a selectivity in the texts considered germane to the issue, and (b) an unwillingness to apply uniformly the same hermeneutic to both the issue of women in the church and the issue of women in marriage.

a. Selectivity in Texts Considered

Egalitarians and traditionalists accuse each other of manipulating the message of Scripture by picking and choosing which aspects of the Biblical record they want to notice. And there often is truth in their assertions. Rather than a consistent, nonpartisan, thorough reading of Scripture which seeks liberation from the pressures of "feminism" and "traditionalism," both sides tend to approach the Bible through a predetermined "interpretive filter."

An obvious example of such filtering is Billy Graham's discussion "Jesus and the Liberated Woman." In the article, Graham discusses the new prestige that Christ brought to women. But using two proof texts, Genesis 3:16 ("To the woman he said, 'I will greatly multiply your pain in childbearing . . .' ") and Titus 2:4–5 ("and so train the young women to love their husbands and children, to be sensible, chaste, domestic, kind, and submissive to their husbands"), he nevertheless concludes: "Wife, mother, homemaker—this is the appointed destiny of real womanhood."[26] Graham overlooks the fact that this is at best a half-truth of Scripture. He has turned the "curse" in Genesis 3:16 into an eternal principle, and has centered on the role of "homemaker" in the text from Titus, to the exclusion of other Scriptural data. Mary, for example, is singled out appreciatively for her unwillingness to be just the homemaker (Luke 10:42). What of Paul's desire that the Corinthians remain single (1 Cor. 7:8)? What, too, of the group of women who left home (and family!) to join Jesus' followers in traveling from town to town with him (Luke 8:2–3; Matt. 27:55)? Again, how is a text like Luke 11:27–28 to be correlated with Graham's assertion that whatever else it describes, the New Testament declares that the "main job" for females is "the womanly assignment of wife and mother"?[27]

> As he [Jesus] said this, a woman in the crowd raised her voice and said to him, "Blessed is the womb that bore you, and the breasts that you sucked!" But he said, "Blessed rather are those who hear the word of God and keep it!" [Luke 11:27–28]

Jesus was not belittling Mary; he was suggesting that real womanhood goes beyond being a wife and mother. Again, it is true that the Bible commands women to bear children. But both mother *and* father are given joint responsibility for the children (cf. Eph. 6:4; Ps. 103:13). Finally, Proverbs 31 describes the ideal wife, it is true. Yet how foreign is its description from Graham's ideal American "homemaker"—purchasing land, acting as a merchant, making "her arms strong." What is our traditional cultural pattern and what is Biblical have been conflated by an editing of the Biblical record.[28]

Such screening of Scripture is found among evangelical feminists as well. Kay Lindskoog, for example, concludes that "Paul's Bad News for Women" is in reality good news. "Surely," she says, "Paul was not endorsing the short-sightedness of his own culture any more than he would endorse the excesses of ours."[29] Unfortunately, when we look more closely at the basis for this conclusion we find it is largely lacking. At first glance she seems to tackle the problem texts for her position. But while purporting to ground her conclusions in a careful exegesis of 1 Timothy 2:8–15 (where women are told to be silent, submissive, and plainly attired), Lindskoog actually limits her discussion of 1 Timothy to pointing up the incongruity of traditional interpretations and concluding, "we must admit that Paul is not his clearest in this passage, to say the least."[30] Concerning 1 Corinthians 14:26–40 (where women are told to keep silence in the churches), Lindskoog limits her remarks to the need for order in the churches, omitting any discussion of Paul's specific injunction regarding women. Her selective analysis of Ephesians 5 points out the need to begin the discussion with verse 21 ("Be subject to one another . . .") and then proceeds to concentrate on verses 25ff., which stress the husband's self-giving love. What is conveniently ignored are verses 22 through 24 which deal with the wife's subjection to her husband.[31] The safest way to be sure Scripture supports your position is to ignore those passages you don't like.[32] Concentrate on "husbands loving your wives" and "doing all things decently and in order" and perhaps others will overlook the fact that you have bypassed injunctions to women to be silent in worship and subject in marriage.

A more sophisticated screening of Scripture is carried out by others who claim that we must look in Scripture for the "locus classicus" of a Biblical doctrine and concentrate on its teaching, interpreting all else in light of its truth. Letha Scanzoni and Nancy Hardesty use this principle fully in their book *All We're Meant to Be:*

> The biblical theologian does not build on isolated proof texts but first seeks the *locus classicus,* the major biblical statement, on a given matter. . . . Passages which deal with an issue systematically are used to help understand incidental references elsewhere. Passages which are theological and doctrinal in content are used to interpret those where the writer is dealing with practical local cultural problems. (Except for Gal. 3:28, all of the references to women in the New Testament are contained in passages dealing with practical concerns about personal relationships or behavior in worship services.)[33]

Here, and in other egalitarian literature, principle is given priority over application; admonition is given preference over description.[34] What is dangerous in such a procedure, though it admittedly works in many cases, is the implied epistemological claim that objective, impersonal statements are of a somehow higher order of trustworthiness than the more personal and relational aspects of Scripture. Do we need systematic argument in order to be fully confident of the meaning of God's revelation? Is it not true that Paul's "purely" theological insights are, on closer inspection, responses to the cultural crises and life situations of young churches facing concrete problems, and that his "purely" practical advice has within it a theological dimension?[35] Paul neither "did theology" in an abstract, academic manner nor "proffered advice" devoid of theological undergirding. Both his "systematic theology" and his "practical theology" are more accurately part of his one and the same "church theology."

The richness and variegation of the New Testament message must be maintained.[36] There is nothing endemic to the text which suggests that "epistle" is a superior form to "Gospel" as a medium for communicating God's truth. An evangelical Biblical theology must listen equally to the theology of the synoptics, of the epistles, of Acts, and even of Old Testament Wisdom literature. The importance of recognizing the authority of multiple Biblical witnesses must be maintained if interpreters are to avoid twisting the Biblical record to support outside aims.[37] Paul Holmer is correct in warning against evangelicals

> treating the Scripture as if it were a literary and metaphysical and casual gloss on a literal and systematic structure that it otherwise hides. The everlasting search among evangelicals for that structure, that is literally true and that is interconnected, makes Scripture often look like an introduction into a better theological scheme that lurks within it.[38]

Such a danger is almost inevitable for those who search out the "locus classicus."[39]

Whether through an arbitrary selectivity concerning which texts are treated, or through a selectivity regarding which aspects of a text are thought relevant, or through a selectivity according to the literary genre and method of presentation, evangelicals on both sides of the controversy concerning woman's rightful role have too often truncated the Scriptural message. In the process, the authority of Scripture has been undercut, the full Biblical message being limited by some predetermined interpretive grid.

b. Inconsistency in the Application of Hermeneutical Procedures

In the interpretation of Biblical themes, selectivity in the texts considered is one danger. A more curious inconsistency is the unwillingness by some evangelicals to apply their hermeneutical method equally to the question of women in the church and to the question of women in the family.

Harold Lindsell, for example, in his book *The World, the Flesh, and the Devil,* finds the position of Paul regarding women exercising leadership and teaching/preaching functions in the church to be an expression of the needs of his cultural situation. It is not to be considered as normative for the church today. He states, furthermore:

> The Bible does speak rather specifically about male-female relationships for those who have been regenerated. Paul is the great advocate of Christian freedom, saying that in Jesus Christ, "There is . . . neither male nor female . . ."

Lindsell concludes that women's roles in the church should not be judged in terms of sexual classification but by "what a particular woman with certain talents, strengths, and weaknesses can do."[40] When he discusses women's role in marriage, however, Lindsell asserts that the Pauline teaching for the Christian requires the husband to be the final authority in decision-making in the home. "The man was made head over the woman (1 Cor. 11:3; Eph. 5:23). . . . that teaching is very strong."[41] On the one hand, Paul's teaching on women in worship is understood to be culturally directed and no longer binding on Christians today; on the other hand, Paul's teaching on women's place in marriage is said to be timeless. Yet the texts reveal that the Pauline arguments are similarly based on (or illustrated with) an analogy with the creation accounts. George Knight is correct:

> This creation order and its correlatives of headship and subjection appear in each passage [dealing with woman's ruling/teaching function in the church] just as they provide the one and only foundation for the role relationships in marriage. To dismiss the role relationships in the church in regard to the teaching/ruling function as simply cultural would carry with it the dismissal of the analogous role relationship in marriage as also cultural. Lindsell is not that consistent; Scanzoni and Hardesty are![42]

A second example of this same unwillingness to carry through on one's method of interpretation to include both facets of the women's question is Gladys Hunt's bestseller, *Ms. Means Myself.* She states her hermeneutical procedure in the preface:

> The rules of biblical interpretation require that we give any passage the obvious meaning the author intended in the context in which he writes. Secondly, Scripture must interpret Scripture.[43]

In chapter two, which is tellingly titled "The Side Issue," Hunt takes up Paul's advice that women should be silent in the church. She begins by painting redemptive history in which male and female were created equal, but in which sin also entered, allowing moral perversion and female discrimination. In Christ, however, woman is again treated as an equal, as Jesus' life, the early church's ministry, and Paul's theology (Gal. 3:28) declare. Furthermore, what inequality there was in the

Biblical world must be contrasted with the stark situation for women among Israel's neighbors. With this Biblical background, Hunt suggests, one can begin to understand Paul's words. But only as (1) the cultural situation Paul addressed, (2) the wider argument in the text, and (3) the other relevant statements by the same author are noted can the interpreter do full justice to Paul's instruction. Moreover, Hunt believes that we cannot be slaves to a faulty church tradition. Doesn't common sense demand that women's gifts be used? Such is an outline of Hunt's argument and her conclusion follows logically: "cultural adjustments" must be made if these texts are to remain meaningful today.[44]

However, when Hunt turns from "The Side Issue" (why is woman's service to God less basic than other of her activities?) to the real thing—the marriage relationship—she forsakes her hermeneutical procedure for a superficial reading of Genesis 2:24 and Ephesians 5:21ff. She concludes that husbands are to lead, and wives are to follow. Because they are "one flesh," they can best operate as an entity in a hierarchical relationship.[45] No reason is provided for this assertion, except the common sense of the interpreter. Aside from the questionableness of this culturally based argument that two people must have a leader, Hunt fails to be convincing because she forsakes her quite adequate method of interpretation for a "literalistic" misunderstanding of the Scriptural text.

A consistent reading of the Biblical record would seem to demand that either an egalitarian or a traditionalist posture be argued in relation both to women in marriage and women in the church. Because all of Scripture is culturally directed—i. e., because all of it was written for a particular situation and out of a particular context—the evangelical cannot use the issue of culture to distinguish between arguments for women's place in marriage and her place in the church. Similarly, the recognition and right use of gifts would prove as applicable a criterion for judging women's suitability for leadership in the family as her suitability for ordination to ministry. A predetermined understanding of woman's rightful roles too often dictates such choices, as well as the more general method of interpretation evangelicals choose. Wanting to question a traditional notion, evangelicals make use of the full range of hermeneutical procedures. Content to maintain the tradition, those same evangelicals at times resort to a simplistic reading of a text that distorts its intended meaning. Consistency, along with a hermeneutical openness, must be an evangelical goal.

Hermeneutics and the Role of Women

The current controversy over women's place in worship and marriage can be healthy for the evangelical church, for only as a position is argued passionately and under pressure are its possibilities fully explored. As long as both sides remain open to new insight, the discussion should spark a testing of tradition and current practice by God's-Word-as-human-words. But such an optimistic prognosis concerning the current debate is dependent on both sides taking their hermeneutical task more seriously. It is necessary, therefore, to sketch out in conclusion some interpretive principles which might assist in answering questions about woman's place in marriage and church.

1. *A text must be treated within its full unit of meaning.* The reference to wives being subject to their husbands (Eph. 5:22–24) can be adequately understood only in terms of the mutual subjection commanded in verse 21, the sacrificial love of the husband prescribed in verses 25–30, and the unity of the marriage partners, verses 31–33. The phrase "be subject to your husbands" depends for its meaning, in other words, on the total scope of verses 21–33. Similarly, 1 Corinthians 14:34–35 is to be understood as part of Paul's summary concerning public worship which begins with verse 26 and continues through verse 40. Seen in this context, Paul's specific advice concerning women not speaking within a worshiping congregation takes on the more primary meaning that all is to "be done decently and in order." (verse 40)

2. *Some translations must be corrected for their sexist bias.* "In the New Testament, masculine nouns and pronouns have often been substituted for the nouns and pronouns of common gender in the original Greek."[46] For example, 1 Timothy 3:1 reads in the King James version: "If a man desire the office of a bishop . . . ." It is better rendered, "If any one desires . . . ." There are other instances of biased translation as well. Phoebe is labeled a "servant" (KJV) in Romans 16:1 and

a "succorer" (KJV; the RSV has "helper") in Romans 16:2, although the first word of description, *diakonos,* is elsewhere usually translated "minister," and the second, *prostatis* (a noun which occurs only this once in the Bible), has a verb form which is translated "rule" or "be over" in other New Testament texts (Rom. 12:8, KJV; 1 Thess. 5:12; 1 Tim. 3:4, KJV; 5:17).[47]

3. *The literary form of a passage must be understood if it is to be adequately interpreted.* We must keep in mind that Gospel and epistle are not sociological tract or disinterested treatise. The very nature of "letters" which were intended to answer specific questions about particular issues in the life of the churches in Corinth and Ephesus (the context of 1 Timothy) should make the reader extremely cautious in deducing universal principles from Paul's advice. Such deductions must stem from an appreciation of the intended meaning of the text which is mediated through specific literary forms. For example, Paul's argument in 1 Corinthians 11 makes use of rabbinic methods of argument common in his day. This fact, when recognized, helps the interpreter focus upon Paul's real intent, while refraining from over-interpreting the "rabbinic" supports Paul includes to buttress his point. A recognition of Paul's methodology does not lead to a dismissal of the text, but to a proper understanding of its meaning.

4. *The historical context of a passage helps the interpreter understand both the function and the meaning a text had in its own day.* Did the actions and words of Jesus and Paul *function* to reinforce the status quo in regard to women, or were they "liberating" even in their own day?[48] When we consider the evident inferior status of women in Biblical times (cf. Ecclus. 42:13–14: "Better is the wickedness of a man than a woman who does good, and it is a woman who brings shame and disgrace"), the meaning of the New Testament's advice to women changes drastically.[49] We must ask whether we are not being unfaithful to the Biblical message if we use Scripture's liberating words to impede the leavening process they were meant to have. As to the *meaning* of a text, it is not proper to give to Biblical language a current-day nuance that was foreign in its day. Consider a word like "head" (*kephale:* 1 Cor. 11:3; Eph. 5:23); if "head" did not have our modern metaphorical sense of "decision-making" in Paul's day, we cannot assign to it that connotation. Again, the meaning of 1 Timothy

2:8–15, which places various restrictions on women's dress and speech, depends not on our context, but on the double background of Paul's Judaism (where women were exempted from learning) and the situation at Ephesus (where untrained women who had submitted to heretical teachers seem to have been seeking to spread their beliefs, perhaps like the *hierodules* in the service of the temple of Diana, cf. 2 Tim. 3:5–7). Rabbinic law and Greek custom, as well as particular situations being addressed, add necessary background and coloring to a correct understanding of the 1 Timothy text.

Also possible is a misuse of the cultural context of a given text. Hardesty and Scanzoni, for example, conclude that the text in Ephesians 5 could not be teaching support for a hierarchical marriage relationship "because the dominant-husband submissive-wife model of marriage was the norm in the societies of that time. There would have been no reason to tell wives to submit to their husbands, or to tell husbands they were the heads."[50] In order to be Pauline, it must be "new," they feel. But surely, Paul could as easily be arguing the need for a return to the regnant pattern after a false application of Christian freedom in the young church as he could be proclaiming that which was at variance with his culture. To accept an interpretation of a text because it is new or distinct from dominant cultural patterns is a faulty hermeneutical procedure.

5. *The immediate context of a passage should be considered before one looks at other parallel texts.* Perhaps a negative example of this principle can be instructive. George Knight, in his discussion in *Christianity Today* on woman's place, finds 1 Corinthians 11:8 and 9 (woman was created "for man") to be of timeless significance.[51] He bases his conclusion on a correlation of that text with Genesis 2:23, 24 and 1 Timothy 2:13. What he fails to consider is the immediate context of these verses (1 Cor. 11:11–12), where Paul qualifies them, lest this phase of his argument regarding women's head coverings be misunderstood. Similarly, in his discussion of 1 Corinthians 14:34 (women keeping silent in the church) in the *Journal of the Evangelical Theological Society,* Knight chooses to turn to 1 Timothy 2:11–14 for his interpretive key ("what is prohibited is teaching with particular reference to men"), rather than to 1 Corinthians 14:40 which summarizes the immediate discussion by commanding that "all things should

be done decently and in order." When he does consider the immediate context, Knight focuses on the preceding argument in verses 27 and 29, rather than on verse 35 which completes Paul's direct advice to women and sets the issue squarely in the context of "asking questions."[52]

6. *The author's explicit intention, methodology, theology, and practice, as understood in other Biblical texts, can provide helpful interpretive clues.* Paul's specific advice concerning women in the church and family can be better understood if it is viewed as part of his larger *intention* to bring order to the Christian community. Only in this way can the church's witness to the wider society avoid being compromised and its life together as a fellowship be strengthened (cf. 1 Tim. 5:14; Tit. 2:5; 1 Cor. 14:33). It is evident from Paul's advice concerning circumcision in 1 Corinthians 7:17–24 that Paul did not see the maintenance of the status quo as a goal of the church. However, it is also clear from his discussion of slavery in Philemon that Paul's *method* for social change was characterized by caution and orderliness. Perhaps Paul's *theological* statement of equality in Christ found in Galatians 3:28 can help the interpreter focus on the particularity and cultural-directedness of other of his advice (e. g., 1 Cor. 14:34–35). Finally, the extensive description of Paul's *ministry* which is found in Acts, as well as the mention of current church *practice* within his epistles, shows Paul's attitude toward women through his action (cf. Acts 16:13; 17:4; Tit. 2:3; 1 Cor. 11:5; Rom. 16:1–16).

7. *The Bible has an overarching consistency despite its multiple theological foci. Thus, all interpretations of given texts can be productively correlated with wider Biblical attitudes, statements, themes, and descriptions.* If husbands are to duplicate Jesus' *attitude* toward leadership (Eph. 5:25ff.; 1 Pet. 3:1), they might consider Matthew 20:25–28:

> "You know that the rulers of the Gentiles lord it over them, and their great men exercise authority over them. It shall not be so among you; but whoever would be great among you must be your servant, and whoever would be first among you must be your slave; even as the Son of man came not to be served but to serve, and to give his life as a ransom for many."

Anyone who finds Paul's advice regarding women to be straightforward and clear might do well to recall the *statement* of 2 Peter 3:16

that there are in Paul's epistles "some things" "hard to understand." In his study *Woman in the Church,* Russell Prohl correctly places his discussion of the specific texts which relate to that issue within the larger Biblical *themes* of creation and redemption.[53] Other Biblical themes, such as the doctrines of God and the church add further insight into the discussion of women's rightful role. For example, though male imagery is predominantly used, nowhere does Scripture suggest (like texts from Israel's neighbors) that God is to be thought of literally as male. Again, if the church as the body of Christ is ordered according to gift rather than gender (1 Cor. 12; Rom. 12; Eph. 4), what is the significance of this fact for female members in our age with the apparent gift of preaching? Finally, the Gospels *describe* women as being significantly involved in declaring the faith (John 4; 20:15–17; Matt. 28:9–10).

8. *Insight into texts which are obscure must be gained from those which are plain.* Here is a key hermeneutical principle for the interpretation of women's place in the church. Ordinarily, hermeneutical procedure would dictate that theologians seeking guidance on this topic should first turn to the three passages which speak directly about this area (1 Tim. 2; 1 Cor. 11; 14). But all of these texts are extremely difficult to interpret: crucial words remain obscure (e. g., *authentein; exousia*); the addressed situations are difficult to reconstruct; the "surface meaning" contradicts other Pauline material; and the methods of argument reflect cultural thought-forms no longer in use. Given these difficulties in interpretation in the texts that seem most appropriate, the plain descriptions of Jesus' interaction with women and the stylized but readily interpreted accounts of woman's creation in Genesis take on increased significance.[54]

9. *Scripture should be read in faith for faith.* The goal of Scripture is to help its reader "put on the Lord Jesus Christ." (Rom. 13:14; Eph. 4:13) Any teaching regarding women must, therefore, square with the truth of the gospel and the world's hope "in Christ." Christ's victory over sin and death has brought with it new possibilities for redeemed humanity. Galatians 3:28 ("there is neither male nor female; for you are all one in Christ Jesus") cannot be used reductively as grounds for dismissing other texts, but neither can it be ignored. Redeemed humanity in the church and Christian marriage should mirror creation's

new order in Christ. Moreover, faith is not only the goal of Biblical interpretation; it is also the means. For as Christians we come humbly and receptively to the text, believing in the Bible's authoritative message for us. A controlled subjectivity is our goal. Our predisposition of faith should allow us to let the text speak normatively in our lives.

10. *Interpreters of Scripture should seek the help of the Christian community, past and present, in order that insights can be shared, humility fostered, and biases of culture and theological tradition overcome.* The Christian community can be wrong in its interpretation of Scripture, as the church's former position on slavery indicates. Only the church, past, present, and future, can correct private presuppositions and cultural bias. Such a correctional process is currently attending the discussion of women in the church and family. Augustine's definition of woman as man's helper in procreation has been rejected by most of the church as sub-Biblical. So too Aquinas's argument for female subordination based on the fact that she is the "weaker vessel," misbegotten and less rational.[55] But to criticize the theology of past generations is relatively painless. To admit the possibility of similar cultural and ecclesiological limitations in ourselves is more difficult. But such seems to be the case presently where those in the Reformed (Knight) and Lutheran (Reumann) traditions remain resistive to women being ordained, while those out of Holiness (Dayton) and Baptist (Lindsell) traditions do not.[56] Has personal background influenced exegesis on this point?[57]

11. *Scriptural interpretation must allow for continuing actualization as necessary implications are drawn out.* What is being claimed here is the fact of *progressive understanding,* not of ongoing revelation. Obvious examples of this need which have surfaced previously are the church's doctrine of the Trinity and the Christian Abolitionist movement. Both are rooted in the Biblical text, though both go beyond it in their exact formulations. They are necessary implications which theological controversy and new cultural situations have brought to light. The changing role of women in the church and family would seem to be another example of this principle. It is no longer a man's world in North America. E.R.A., birth control, Title IX, and the like, have brought a new consciousness of women's rights and possibilities to the contemporary Christian. Given this outside stimulus, the

church has begun to reevaluate its stance toward women. A key aspect in this is the hermeneutical task of setting forth Scripture's implications for women *in our day.* Those opposed to change claim that culture has determined the church's interpretation of the Biblical text. Although this is true in some cases, it need not follow from taking one's context seriously. Instead of being determinative of its interpretation, culture can serve the church by being the occasion for renewed reflection and debate. A progressive understanding of Scripture should be continual as situations alter, allowing new implications of the text to come to light.

Conclusion

Does such a critical, yet faithful, approach as that outlined above imply that only the expert can arrive at an adequate Biblical understanding of the role of women in the church and family? It is true that evangelicals, following after the Reformers, confess the clarity (or "perspicuity") of Scripture. But by this, they do not mean an "objective" clarity which demands no interpretation or translation. Rather they seek to emphasize by this creedal stance that Scripture's purpose —its message of salvation—is accessible to all and is not limited to the clergy.

The need remains for ongoing work in interpreting Scripture, if the Bible is to be normative. Our discussion above has highlighted this fact in regard to the issue of woman's role. Such reflection is necessitated not only because of our own faulty frames of reference, but also because God's Word comes to us in the concrete form of historical language (which is not always self-evident). Moreover, such interpretation, if it is to prove fruitful, must be based on a correct methodology, i. e., an adequate hermeneutic. This chapter has sought to address this need. Receptive attention and faithful research must have an adequate methodological undergirding. Although Scripture is available to all and sufficient unto salvation for those who read attentively, a proper hermeneutic is necessary so that private interpretations can be corrected and fresh stimulus gained for the ongoing theological task of the church.

As we turn in the next chapter to consider the evangelical church's role in society, we will see that matters of a correct theological understanding of social ethics—one resting in Biblical authority—do not hinge so much on the issue of Biblical hermeneutics as they do on the matter of conflicting loyalties to ecclesiological traditions. Just as evangelicals have reached an impasse in their Biblical understanding of woman's role in the church and family because of an inadequate methodology for interpreting Scripture, so evangelicals have failed to reach a consensus in their discussions of social ethics because of their various commitments to differing theological traditions. To ask whether evangelicals are Dispensational, Reformed, or Anabaptist is to discover in most instances their understanding of the church's role in the social arena as well. Therefore, where attention to hermeneutical concerns has dominated the constructive suggestions of this chapter, an evaluation of the direction a dialogue between the competing theological traditions must take will provide the following chapter its overall direction.

As the first chapter indicated, constructive evangelical theology is a dynamic blend of Biblical, traditional, and contemporary sources, all operating in such a way as to insure the continued place of Scripture as one's final authority. In practice, this will lead to different emphases and approaches on each new topic. On the issue of women, evangelical theologians must give more attention to hermeneutical concerns. In chapter V, we will note that an evangelical answer to the question of homosexuality centers at the point of the church's interaction with contemporary society. Regarding matters of social ethics, it is the interaction between competing traditions that holds out the most promise for helping evangelicals to move beyond their current impasse.

IV

Evangelical Social Ethics: The Use of One's Theological Tradition

In his book *Evangelicalism and Social Responsibility,* Vernon Grounds, the president of Conservative Baptist Seminary in Denver, sketches the following caricature of evangelicals concerning their social indifference and ineffectiveness.[1] He states that evangelicals can be criticized for their *conservatism*—they sanctify the status quo; for their *quietism*—they naively trust Providence to remedy social injustice; for their *pietism*—their concern is with one's soul, not concrete needs; for their *perfectionism*—only the unqualifiedly good can be supported; for their *legalism*—righteousness applies more to abstinence than to paying employees livable wages; for their *nationalism* —the essence of the American way of life is thought to be Christian; and for their *pessimism*—only the end of the age will bring hope.

David Moberg is similarly critical:

> We [evangelicals] wait until there is general consensus in society before we speak on controversial issues in a pattern of "me-too-ism" that makes us almost like contemporary ancestors of the present generation. We focus upon personal vices and individual problems, failing to see that the great sweeping social problems of our time also are personal problems for all their victims. We defend "the rights of property" when they clash with the physical, psychological, or intellectual welfare of underprivileged people. We hail the class-related positions of the rich with rationalizing Scripture passages and salve our consciences for neglecting the poor by giving out a few Thanksgiving baskets and making token contributions to a gospel mission. If our neighborhood begins to deteriorate and

poor whites or Negroes begin to invade it, we move our homes
and churches to the suburbs . . . and thus we betray our Lord.[2]

Such are caricatures surely, but evangelicals and non-evangelicals
alike recognize familiar lines in the drawings. Evangelicals stand ac-
cused, by those within as well as without, of uninvolvement and/or
wrong involvement on the major issues of social justice in our day.

Viewed historically such assessments have strong validity. One
can find numerous examples like William Brenton Greene, Jr. who in
1912 argued that the more acute the social crisis, the more the church
needed to emphasize its own mission of evangelism.[3] Greene believed
that no crisis outshone the religious crisis and there was neither time
nor energy to go in two directions. Moreover, argued Greene, even if
it wanted to, the church could not effectively enter into social service,
for it lacked the required exact and varied knowledge. The early
church recognized its limitations in this area and was able thus to be
of influence where it counted.

But the historical example of a Greene can be countered today
with a host of evangelical voices ranging from Billy Graham to John
Warwick Montgomery, from Robert Linder and Richard Pierard to
Mark Hatfield, from Sherwood Wirt to Bill Bright to Richard Quebedeaux.[4] Evangelicals have awakened to the need for a whole gospel.
The unbridgeable dichotomies which Greene expressed between salvation and service, between proclamation and demonstration, between faith and works are beginning to give way. In their place is the
widespread recognition expressed by Billy Graham that "Jesus taught
that we are to take regeneration in one hand and a cup of cold water
in the other."[5]

Carl F. H. Henry's *The Uneasy Conscience of Modern Fundamentalism* was certainly the key document in evangelicalism's emerging
social conscience. Written in 1947, the book bemoaned the needless
assault fundamentalism was undergoing for refusing to apply "the
genius of our position [i. e., the orthodox faith] constructively to those
problems which press most for solution in a social way." In its revolt
against the Social Gospel, evangelical Christianity had become unwit-
tingly inarticulate about the social reference of the gospel. Henry
therefore declared:

If historic Christianity is again to compete as a vital world ideology, evangelicalism must project a solution for the most pressing world problems. It must offer a formula for a new world mind with spiritual ends, involving evangelical affirmations in political, economic, sociological, and educational realms, local and international. The redemptive message has implications for all of life; a truncated life results from a truncated message.[6]

In his book, Henry did not spell out the implications of this challenge to the church, but his clarion was loud and clear. As Billy Graham echoed six years later: "Christians, above all other, should be concerned with social problems and social injustice."[7]

That evangelicals should be involved socially has become a foregone conclusion. As John Montgomery states, the effort to validate Christian social concern is "tantamount to a statistical survey demonstrating that all husbands are married, or a search purporting to discover who is buried in Grant's tomb."[8] But *how* and *why* evangelicals are to involve themselves in society have proven to be much more vexing questions. That they are to be involved brings near unanimity; how that involvement takes shape and what is its Christian motivation bring only debate. As Henry himself recently characterized the situation, evangelicals are increasingly divided "over what program Christian social ethics implies."[9] Judy Brown Hull, co-chairperson of Evangelicals for Social Action, a coalition which first met in 1973 in Chicago over the Thanksgiving holiday, echoes a similar appraisal: "justice-minded evangelicals are squaring off against each other," she bemoans.[10]

One such dispute that has surfaced is a difference between the editors of *Sojourners* and the editors of *The Reformed Journal*, two leading evangelical periodicals. In a series of articles and editorials that appeared in both magazines during 1977, differences of opinion over the church's involvement in society were defined and debated with little resolution.[11] Although both sides refrained from labeling it merely a contemporary version of the debate between sixteenth-century Anabaptism and sixteenth-century Calvinism, both recognized the importance their historical antecedents played in the discussion. *In fact, it can be argued (and I will, in what follows below) that the present divergences in social thought throughout contemporary evangelicalism stem largely from this source—from differing theological traditions that provide conflicting models for social ethics today.* Evangelical social ethics reflects in its diversity the variety of theological perspectives out of which evangelicalism springs, a variety which includes among others, American revivalism and fundamentalism, as well as Anabaptism and Calvinism.[12]

Evangelicals must take with increased seriousness the variety of traditions from which they spring, for here is one major source of conflict in their present theological formulations. Here, also, is a major resource for theological consensus-building. Where the resolution of conflict over the proper shape of Biblical hermeneutics surfaced as central for an evangelical consensus in its understanding of the role of women, the use of tradition as a theological resource holds promise for evangelicals as they seek to move beyond their current impasse regarding social ethics. If evangelicalism's commitment to social activity (care? concern? action? responsibility? welfare? justice? —the lack of a consensus even at this basic level of vocabulary hints at the problem) is to prove productive; and more important, if its theoretical commitment to Biblical authority is to maintain its integrity by proving true in practice; then evangelicals must learn to use the insights of their theological past to build a Biblically based social ethic relevant to today.

How can evangelicals mine the resources of their divergent Christian heritages, while maintaining their commitment to Biblical authority? A dialogue between the conflicting theological perspectives provides the key. Evangelicals must be willing to have their long-standing social beliefs enriched and/or challenged by fellow evangelicals who similarly accept Scripture as authoritative, but who interpret it according to opposing theological models. They must find in the insights of other evangelicals a stimulus for a renewed investigation of the Biblical data. And they must be willing to draw out new conclusions theologically from their clarified Biblical perspective as it interacts with contemporary understandings in society.

In the remainder of this chapter, I will suggest the general shape which such a programmatic might take regarding social ethics. I will turn, first, to a description of a variety of evangelical perspectives concerning social ethics. Having listened to these positions and ob-

served the importance which theological traditions play in their formulations, I will then look for direction as to how a renewed investigation of the Biblical data might proceed. In this case, I will find a major
resource for theological consensus-building in a Biblical definition of
"social justice." Although there is much work still to be done on this
topic, I believe there is sufficient clarity in present Biblical scholarship
to risk such a definition. Using the concept of "social justice" as a key,
I will then seek to draw out the implications of this Biblical perspective for an evangelical social ethic through a series of questions.

If further study reveals that modifications must be made in the
proposed concept of "social justice" in order for it to remain true to
the Biblical witness, some of the conclusions of this chapter will no
doubt be changed. But its general shape as to theological methodology
will not. And here is my primary interest. The current impasse in
evangelicalism over social ethics provides us a model for exploring
how a dialogue between conflicting theological traditions can aid
theological formation as evangelicals seek to apply concretely their
theoretical commitment to Biblical authority.

A Cross Section of Current Evangelical Opinion
Concerning Social Responsibility

In sketching a cross section of current approaches to social ethics
within the evangelical church, numerous approaches are possible. But
perhaps as representative a procedure as any is to use as paradigms
of current evangelical diversity four of evangelicalism's leading periodicals—*Moody Monthly, Christianity Today, The Reformed Journal,*
and *Sojourners.* These journals have been selected for they reflect not
only a breadth of current evangelical thought, but a range of the
traditions undergirding contemporary evangelicalism as well. The
magazines move from the strongly traditional viewpoint of *Moody
Monthly* (a viewpoint carrying on the social ethic of late nineteenth-
century American revivalism), through the moderately conservative
stance of *Christianity Today* (a stance that seeks perhaps uncon-
sciously to revive the social activism of American fundamentalism
prior to the repeal of Prohibition and the Scopes trail), to the socially
liberal commitment of *The Reformed Journal* (a position seeking to

be contemporary, and yet faithful to Calvin's thought) and the socially radical perspective of *Sojourners* (a perspective molded in the Anabaptist tradition).

1. Moody Monthly

Perhaps the most popular periodical among Dispensational evangelicals is *Moody Monthly.* Reflecting the basic orientation of its namesake, the late nineteenth-century evangelist Dwight L. Moody, as well as that of the school he established, Moody Bible Institute in Chicago, the journal has as its main concern the task of evangelism —that is, the preparation for, understanding of, reporting about, and inciting interest in the proclamation of the gospel. Moreover, as it warned in an editorial on the 1974 International Congress on World Evangelization in Lausanne, evangelism must not be confused with the Christian responsibility for genuine social concern. " 'To evangelize is to spread the good news that Jesus Christ died for our sins and was raised from the dead according to the Scriptures, and that He now offers the forgiveness of sins and the liberating gift of the Spirit to all who repent and believe.' "[13]

But although evangelism is understood as being the Christians', as well as this journal's, primary responsibility, Christian social responsibility is not ignored. As contributing editor Howard Whaley states, the aim of evangelicals is "to prevent indifference to social issues on the one hand, yet avoid social gospel pitfalls on the other."[14] Seeking to carry out this goal through its editorials and articles, the magazine points to three aspects of Christian social responsibility: (a) the importance of spiritual renewal, (b) the necessity of ministry through benevolences, and (c) the need for responsible, Biblically principled citizenship.

The need for a spiritual awakening in America is an oft-recurring theme in the *Moody Monthly.* "It's no secret that America is sick," states executive editor George Sweeting, who is also president of Moody Bible Institute. "But few realize that her one hope lies in the ends of God's people." If America is to survive, it must have a revival —a regaining of spiritual consciousness—beginning with the church itself. Until God's people are broken, until they prayerfully repent and turn in radical commitment to the Lord, the nation will continue to flounder. "Let's stir up the gift that God has planted in us and seek the outpouring from heaven that our nation and our day so greatly need!"[15]

In addition to emphasizing serious Christian commitment and discipleship, the monthly stresses voluntary service to the needy, both materially and spiritually. The avowed goal of all such benevolent activity is the demonstration of the gospel. Articles and editorials on emergency world relief, hunger, poverty, friendship to the POWs, care for the elderly, homosexuality, ministry to the hurts of the inner city, and the like appear regularly in the magazine's pages. In the vast majority of these articles and editorials, the social issue is discussed as a prelude to the larger issue of evangelism. From out of the apparent physical anguish, dislocation, or hardship, the editors see a greater spiritual need which must be addressed in and through the material one.

The third prong of the Christian's social responsibility in addition to costly discipleship and generous, evangelistically oriented benevolence is Biblically principled citizenship. Because the Bible tells Christians to honor those in authority, they must do so. This does not mean, however, a blanket endorsement of American policy: "When America is right, we support her. When America is wrong, we still love her—and do our best to correct her," states editor Sweeting.[16] For *Moody Monthly* this has meant speaking out editorially or in articles against abortion, welfare, the E.R.A., détente with Russia, the corruption of Watergate, pornography, state lotteries, leniency in homosexuality laws, and euthanasia. It means speaking on behalf of the death penalty, racial equality, and American aid to Israel. The Christian citizen should call on government to enforce Scriptural mandates and to limit itself to its preservative function in society. This can best happen if individual Christians act by writing their elected officials, by voting justly, and by praying.

Behind such a programmatic is an underlying acceptance of the structure of American society. Even when the structure proves glaringly inadequate, as in the energy crisis of 1974, the monthly does not offer significant social critique. Instead it editorializes by drawing spiritual object lessons from the economic crisis, by reminding us that we can see in the situation our need for dependence on God, and by admonishing us to be thankful to God it is not any worse than it is.[17]

Cautious, selective, Biblically based social engagement, qualified by the more basic concern for spiritual renewal, motivated by compassion toward the needy and the opportunity for evangelism, and actualized by responsible individual citizenship and benevolence characterizes *Moody Monthly*'s social ethics. The journal, thus, can be seen as carrying on the individualistic, pietistic shape of its founder's social ministry. It represents the conservative wing of evangelical social engagement.

2. Christianity Today

While Carl Henry served as editor of *Christianity Today*, the editorial policy of what has become the Christian community's largest circulating periodical mirrored his position. Spelled out in a lengthy lead editorial entitled "Evangelicals in the Social Struggle," as well as in books such as *Aspects of Christian Social Ethics*, Henry's understanding of Christian social responsibility stressed (a) society's need for the spiritual regeneration of all men and women, (b) an interim social program of humanitarian care, ethical proclamation, and personal, structural application, and (c) a theory of limited government centering on certain "freedom rights," e. g., the rights to public property, free speech, and so on.[18] Though the shape of this social ethic thus closely parallels that of the present editorial position of *Moody Monthly*, it must be distinguished from its counterpart by the time period involved (it pushed others like *Moody Monthly* into a more active involvement in the social arena), by the intensity of its commitment to social responsibility, by the sophistication of its insight into political theory and practice, and by its willingness to offer structural critique on the American political system.

But *Christianity Today* has moved away from the position of its founder on matters of social concern. It has, on the one hand, become more in line with the American way of life, while at the same time increasing its commentary and critique on specific social and political issues. A loose parallel might helpfully be drawn between the magazine's changes and the development of revivalism into fundamentalism, prior to fundamentalism's retrenchment in the social arena following the debacle of the Scopes trial and the

repeal of Prohibition. For fundamentalism, from within its individualistic and pietistic commitments, did for a time frontally
challenge the evil structures of its day, even while remaining
strongly patriotic. Here, too, is *Christianity Today*'s programmatic.

Since Harold Lindsell assumed the position of editor late in the
sixties, *Christianity Today* has moved away from the mere elucidation
of socially related Biblical principles, as Henry thought was right, to
an ongoing commitment to social critique and specific commentary on
a wide range of social and political issues. Rather than leave specific
policy assessment to individual Christians, the editors have sought to
provide informed opinion for their readership. Thus, in a period from
1972 to 1977, of the better than 700 editorials in the magazine, more
than one-third involved public issues. *Christianity Today*'s favorite
topic during this period was its anti-abortion campaign. This, along
with its ongoing assessment of Watergate and its call for American
political pressure against Russia's persecution of Christians, was a
repeated focus of it editorials.

The magazine's strong Christian lobby has also ranged from Vietnam to postal rates, from gun control (pro) to child abuse (con), from
amnesty (a la Ford) to television programming to crime in the streets.
If one were to generalize on the nature of the topics addressed, one
would note a marked focus on questions of individual morality,
human rights, and strong, limited government. But the range of issues
addressed belies somewhat the caricature of conservative Christians
as being involved in only a select number of social issues.

Qualifying its vigorous social commentary has been *Christianity
Today*'s belief that "a spiritual awakening and a turn to Judeo-
Christian principles is the sole hope left to the Western world."[19] "The
nation needs regenerated people, and this is the business of 'revivalism'; and it needs keepers of the Law of God, which is at the heart
of a pietism that emphasizes ethical absolutes."[20] Here is a view of the
church's essential social mandate that parallels early, socially active
fundamentalism. The church collectively is not to work for politico-
economic liberation as the Social Gospel movement argued, and as the
World Council of Churches now believes, but first of all is to foster
individual salvation and personal holiness.

Because all people do not respond to the preaching of the gospel and its concomitant call to discipleship, however, the gospel itself demands that Christians both encourage society to " 'make serious and positive use of the social theories' of Jesus Christ and the Scriptures," and help society to heal social injustices by loving our neighbors as ourselves.[21] Toward this end, the church must first of all proclaim to the world the Bible's perfect rule not only for faith but also for *practice*. State the editors, "Those who know and practice . . . truth must ever stand as guardians of what is essentially the Christian tradition, and call before the bar of human justice and public opinion those who traduce these truths of natural and special revelation."[22]

Active social reform (or involvement in the structures of society) will follow such proclamation, but it will be left by and large to concerned individuals.[23] According to the editors, individual Christian involvement will include responsible public criticism of the errors of government (e. g., détente, price freezing, opposition to capital punishment, corrupt leadership, lack of low-rent housing) while remaining always orderly and loyal in the process. Christians, moreover, should seek specific legislation where appropriate (e. g., regulations of nursing homes, censorship of pornography, prohibition of state casinos), while encouraging non-governmental solutions whenever feasible (e. g., child abuse counseling centers, voluntary contributions to the arts).

In addition to fleshing out a Christian social theory, individual Christians must continue to participate in voluntary social programs of benevolence—inside the church and without. "Those of us who are Christians—and who, for the most part, live in wealthy and favored nations," writes the editor, "should deprive ourselves of our luxuries and surpluses and do all that we can to alleviate the worst suffering of our fellow humans."[24]

Christianity Today's advice to concerned individual Christians includes direct socio-political opinion and action, as well as a recognition of the need for generous benevolence. But though we work to remedy or alleviate certain temporal societal ills, the editors believe that social service and/or political change can never provide society's ultimate answer given human sin. For this reason, government should be severely restricted, beyond its necessary role in defense and citizens' rights protection. Government social programs are not the pana-cea: they usually end up hurting more than they help; they often lack proper controls; and they inevitably lead to fiscal irresponsibility. It is not big government, but Jesus Christ alone who "has a solution for the mess into which man has got himself."[25]

Nevertheless, though our political and economic system is imper-fect, Christians can remain thankful for it. "As is often quoted our democracy is the worst system in history, except for every other one that has ever been tried," the editors declare.[26] Similarly capitalism is viewed as being more just than socialism/Marxism (the two are equated). Though they want to criticize government for the sake of reforming it, the editors deny any need for basic societal restructur-ing.[27] It was this basic trust in the American system which caused *Christianity Today* to accept the president's word concerning Water-gate—until Cox's firing and the tapes— and to back the president concerning his role in Vietnam as late as May 1972:

> Whether we approve or disapprove of the President's con-duct of the war, we are going to have to live with what he has chosen to do . . . . However, the people will have their say in November. . . . Christians should stand by the President, even if they think his policy is mistaken. Every Christian should pray that what is being done will lead to peace and justice.[28]

The editors of *Christianity Today* have chosen to support the American political system, becoming a strong Christian political lobby within it. Qualifying this role, however, is a recognition that all governmental solutions are imperfect, and personal holiness and indi-vidual salvation remain our nation's only ultimate hope. The journal's social stance, therefore, has become an interim policy centering on benevolence, social critique, and limited social reform. Their position remains basically a conservative one within the social arena.

3. The Reformed Journal

The Reformed Journal is edited by a team who are all members of the Christian Reformed Church. Though its immediate constitu-ency is narrow, the magazine's cogent manner in addressing theology from an evangelical, Calvinist perspective has given it significant influ-ence throughout evangelicalism and beyond. Although there is some variety in the editorial position reflected in the journal, the editorializing of theologian and social ethicist Lewis Smedes is perhaps representative.

While not downplaying the significance of evangelism, Smedes opposes the assumption which we have seen represented in *Moody Monthly* and *Christianity Today* that somehow "good men [i. e., Christians] will make good societies." Personal redemption is vital. Moreover, no society is going to be good without good people. But to make individual evangelism the priority for one's social ethics is naive according to Smedes.[29] (Changed people don't always change laws.) Along with evangelism, the church needs to recognize life's corporate nature and to involve itself directly in social and political structures. Referring approvingly to Mark Hatfield's commencement address in 1970 at Fuller Seminary, Smedes states in an editorial:

> Unless Christians recognize that structures can work iniquity as well as justice, they will wash their zeal in frustration as they try to reform American society by reforming individuals. . . . the Christian must be aware that if he is to be effective, he too—in his own, constructive but radical way—has to tend to the economic, political, and social structure.[30]

Social ethics means concrete "political" engagement for the Christian. Such structural involvement will be a complement to the church's task of evangelism.

Most conservative evangelicals have slowly and inconsistently recognized the need for such political involvement, usually in areas touching on individual sin—pornography, corrupt politicians, sexual practices, drugs, abortion on demand, crime, and so forth. But systemic sin, according to Smedes, has more often and wrongfully been ignored. The large hardcore areas of social deprivation—the dislocations and hardships brought on people by shifts in economic and social patterns—are matters which a Christian social ethic must address.[31] Why is it that civil rights are championed while economic rights are ignored?

Traditionally, the evangelical response to structural injustice in the socio-economic sector has been benevolence. While Smedes and the other editors of *The Reformed Journal* do not deny the need or desirability of Christian acts of compassion, they argue that structural violence demands social redress that goes beyond benevolence, being based first of all in the human rights of the victims. If it is right to seek political solutions in certain personal areas of life, why not in the whole range of life's experiences? Certainly Christ is the Lord of "all things." (Eph. 1:22)

It is at this point that Smedes becomes more cautious than other of his colleagues on *The Reformed Journal*'s editorial staff. Though silence and noninvolvement on the one hand, or simple benevolence on the other, are not options for the church as it confronts society's crucial affairs, neither is an "unwarranted meddling."[32] How is the Christian to distinguish what constitutes meddling? Smedes is not altogether clear. He tries to distinguish between the church's declarations of concrete, Biblically based moral principle (this is its rightful task) and its statements on political policy (this is the province of the government). The church speaks corporately, concretely, and constructively about public issues where moral dimensions are prominent, but it does not move beyond moral valuation to issue political directives. "The Church has to find its way between airy generalities and particular policies," Smedes writes. "It must speak with the authenticity of biblical principle without becoming innocently abstract. It must speak to the concreteness of the present situation without taking on the posture of a heavenly State Department."[33]

To give a concrete example of this distinction, in the July-August 1967 edition of *The Reformed Journal* Smedes stated his position forcefully that America's presence in Vietnam was immoral on Biblical grounds (cf. *Moody Monthly* and *Christianity Today,* which remained at least tacit supporters of government policy throughout the war). But unlike some of his socially liberal colleagues, Smedes refrained from advising Dean Rusk how he should end America's presence in the war.[34] Smedes does not seem to be totally consistent at this point, however. In another editorial he argues that the church should promote such concrete programs as Social Security, Medicare, the Jobs Corps, and the massive attack on the intolerable slums of our great cities.[35] These are concrete applications of Scripture's moral principles, viewed in light of contemporary social and economic reality.

Behind editor Smedes's call for the church to involve itself in the whole range of life's experiences, including the socio-political sector, is a strong notion of "social justice." Again, Smedes and his editorial associates diverge here from their more conservative colleagues. For Smedes, justice involves the right for all persons to share in the common goods.[36] To be able to provide for your family, to live where you can afford a house, to have access to adequate health care and public accommodations, these are rights that all possess by reason of their God-appointed humanity. Government, as an agent of justice, must therefore move beyond protection and deterrent functions to the active and creative promotion of human rights.

Smedes, like Calvin, understands the government to function as an agent of justice in a way analogous to the father in a family: "The father has to do more than keep the kids out of each other's hair. He has the task of providing for the welfare of each child and not as a matter of charity, but of right."[37] Here then is the motivation for Smedes's social agenda—a corporate, familial sense of human justice governmentally based.

Smedes is not a Pollyanna in his expectations for achieving social justice; but neither is he fatalistic. *The Reformed Journal* editor recognizes that suffering will be the necessary style of the Christian's entire life.[38] Just as God entered fully into history in the Christ-event, taking upon himself its pain, so Christians must commit themselves to the human situation, assuming its misery. To do this is neither uncreative morbidity nor neurotic self-flagellation. Instead, it is faithful obedience to Christ's agenda for transforming this world. In the life, death, and resurrection of Jesus, we discover that this battle for justice has been won. It is therefore with an eschatological hope that we act, remaining confident of the meaningfulness of our social agenda. Writes Smedes:

> Realistic, to be sure; we are not going to build the Kingdom of God. But despairing, never. We should have no illusions; the hope is centered on God and not on human programs for renewal. But it is a hope in God that makes human programs meaningful and responsible.[39]

Here then is a "reformist" social ethic in the tradition of Calvin himself. Stressing the endeavor for social justice as a complement to the task of evangelism, recognizing the inadequacy of benevolences to meet the challenge, and therefore seeking concrete, structural, political involvement based on a Biblically informed concept of "social justice," editor Smedes argues that the church's action will "find its way on the ridge between harmless generalities and divisive particularities."[40] It will be sacrificial yet hopeful, realistic and engaged.

4. Sojourners

Sojourners (formerly called the *Post American*) gives voice to another opinion in evangelicalism concerning social ethics, one increasingly being felt by the wider community. First published in 1971 by a staff who were largely Trinity Evangelical Seminary students, the magazine has become increasingly clear in its orientation. Articulated by editor Jim Wallis in his book *Agenda for Biblical People,* as well as by editorials and articles by the staff, the *Sojourners* position reflects a Christian radicalism steeped in the Anabaptist tradition—one committed to rigorous discipleship, corporate life-style, and societal critique.

Central to the magazine's concern is its desire to explore fully the implications of the Lordship of Jesus Christ. For the editors, and for the intentional community within which they live, Jesus' life is politically axiomatic. They believe, therefore, that Jesus neither calls his people to a personal, individualistic salvation, nor to a life of secular commitment to social action and class struggle, but rather to a participation with him in the kingdom of God. It is Jesus who defines "the new order of the kingdom of God in the midst of the old order of this world," states Wallis.[41] This new order is set against all secular orders, being based on repentance and issuing forth in sacrificial, obedient common life. Seeking separation from the world's power, the church derives its total orientation, including its positive social ethic, not "out of examples or out of the cases and circumstances," but only concretely from "the revelation of God in Jesus Christ."[42] It is thus an *imitatio Christi* (an imitation of Christ in all things) which informs the *Sojourners* editorial position; it seeks "to accept the political example and style of Jesus."[43]

Seeking to live solely by the values and priorities of Jesus Christ and his kingdom, desiring, that is, to be Christ's community of called-out people, the *Sojourners* staff and community have sought (a) to become post-American in their social critique, visibly protesting the systems of death in the world. They have understood (b) the key to God's action in history to be in the common life of his sojourning community. And they have recognized (c) the need to be in daily involvement with the poor, believing that the church's orientation within society must be informed by the powerless and dispossessed.

Sojourners is suspicious of, if not downright opposed to, all expressions of society based on political power and governmental institutions. Because all secular structures are demonically influenced, because all forms of power breed their own abuse of the poor and powerless, because the use of power not only invites, but demands, compromise with evil—Christians must distance themselves from the public political arena. But this is all right, for "the state is never intended to be an instrumentality for bringing in the new order."[44] Conservative and liberal Christian political agendas are equally mistaken (*The Reformed Journal* and *Christianity Today* are equally in error). Neither a blind conformity to the American way of life nor a naive commitment to society's reconstitution by reforms of political power and institutionalism are adequate socio-political positions for the follower of Jesus. Social justice can only be achieved through a Biblically based response to the poor, hungry, and oppressed, centering on the counter ethic of the kingdom of God as realized in the called-out community. As coeditor Wes Michaelson states:

> My experience [he was Mark Hatfield's chief legislative assistant for several years] is that when you get involved in the political order, you then are asked continually to compromise, relegate, reinterpret, or dismiss central New Testament teachings in order to preserve your own place within the order, or to preserve the government itself on the terms which it defines. To gain power within the system, I have to play according to its rules which are part of a fallen order, directly in contradiction to the kingdom that I have given my life to.[45]

Christians are to be post-American. They are sojourners, aliens in a strange land; their task is that of demythologizing and debunking all ideological idolatry (whether Marxism or capitalism, liberal democracy or conservatism).[46]

Committed only to Jesus Christ and his kingdom, Christians must not only challenge the present church's socio-political involvement (whether reformist or conservative), they must also take as their first priority the rebuilding of the church. Here is Christ's kingdom made concrete. Here is the Christian's rightful "political" mission. To act in terms of the kingdom is to become a new order—a new community living out a common life together. Thus the strong economic and political critique of American and world-wide power is balanced in the pages of *Sojourners* by an increasingly strong commitment to a communitarian Christian life-style. "It is our belief," writes Wallis, "that authentic political existence requires an authentic personal and communal existence."[47] The focus on community is not interpreted as an act of withdrawal from the "political" task or a substitution for involvement. It is instead the outworking of a basic understanding of Christ's kingdom as one that is a countersign to the established powers and structures. Just as Jesus rejected both the politics of the Sadducees and the revolutionary violence of the Zealots, so his followers must embody not with their weapons but with their lives a counter social ethic. "Change comes, we suspect," states Wallis, "more through the witness of creative and prophetic minorities who refuse to meet the system on its own terms but rather act out of an alternative social vision upon which they have based their lives."[48]

Seeking society's transformation by embodying an alternate "political" structure—a new communal order based in the kingdom of God, the people of *Sojourners* have understood that the social location of their church must be alongside the poor and dispossessed. A comparison with *Christianity Today* can be instructive at this point. *Christianity Today*'s board chairman, Harold Ockenga, announced in 1977 that that magazine would move to a suburb of Wheaton, Illinois because " 'Deleterious things happen to attitudes if a person lives here' " in Washington, D.C., amid the moral decay of soaring liquor consumption and illegitimate births.[49] *Sojourners,* on the other hand, recently chose to relocate its intentional community and editorial offices in the heart of that same capital district, amid the suffering and dispossessed. The church must be involved daily with the poor, Wallis believes, for the Christian community is called Biblically to look at the systems of the world through the eyes of their victims. Joined in community with the poor, the church can be a visible protest and confrontation with the forces of death at work in the world today. Committed to the urban neighborhood, *Sojourners* is involved not only in political organizing and lobbying, but in food cooperatives, dayschool tutoring programs, neighborhood recreational programs, and extended-family living situations. The *Sojourners* involvement mirrors its commitment to "stand outside" the system of power and to "stand alongside" those who are powerless.

Providing a radical critique of all political power and a living, eschatological model of the coming kingdom, *Sojourners* has committed itself to a common life of servanthood alongside the poor as an alternate mode of political effectiveness.

Some Questions Evangelicals Must Face

What sense can be made of the editorial policies of the journals described above? The spectrum of evangelical opinion concerning social ethics which these periodicals define could perhaps be sharpened by further explication of the positions of representative individual Christians. Even more radically conservative, though somewhat aligned with *Moody Monthly*'s position, for example, is Rus Walton's. His bicentennial book *One Nation Under God* advocated generous benevolence by the rich to the poor, out of the overflow of their resources, stemming from the free enterprise system and made possible by our republican ("Christian") constitution.[50] More radical in his critique of America's unjust structures, but less willing than the current editors of *Christianity Today* for the church to become directly involved in social and political policy (only "in some emergency") has been Carl F. H. Henry. Like the editors of *The Reformed Journal,* evangelical sociologist David O. Moberg has sought a better balance between personal evangelism and social action, and between Biblical principle and social reality (as understood by the social sciences).[51] Finally, Senator Mark O. Hatfield could be mentioned as a strong ally of the *Sojourners* political stance of Christian protest and suffering servanthood, though his periodic desires to flee politics in order to work for the principles of the kingdom have so far been modified by his partial success in working to bring about God's justice within the American political arena.[52]

If space allowed for further delineation of the social ethics of these representative evangelicals, it would prove illuminating. But whether evangelicalism is surveyed by an assessment of the editorial policies of its leading periodicals, or whether it is understood by reference to various of its leading spokespersons, the fact of evangelicalism's wide range of opinion in regard to social ethics cannot be gainsaid. It is this very breadth of current opinion that is perhaps the most important single characteristic defining contemporary evangelicalism's social stance.

While such diversity might be expected among Christian groups where pluralistic approaches to theological authority are knowingly taken, it is difficult to reconcile within a body which claims the Bible as its sole authorizing agent. The lack of consensus within the evangelical community in regard to a Christian social ethic suggests that there exists within evangelicalism an inability to translate a theoretical commitment to Biblical authority into practice. The problem, as in the previous chapters, is the lack of an adequate interpretive procedure for making the Bible truly authoritative within contemporary evangelical theology. Largely in opposition to their conscious desire, evangelicals have let other standards besides Scripture function authoritatively in their theological and ethical social formulations. In particular, they have found authorization for their social ethics in the distinct, but conflicting theological traditions in which their respective Christian communities reside. Given multiple communities, and thus multiple theological traditions, we discover multiple ethical formulations.

That contemporary evangelical ideas of social ethics are rooted in outside theological/ideological frameworks can perhaps be illustrated by comparing the four positions outlined above with that of California politics over the last twenty years. What we have in evangelical social ethics is a rough analogue of the ideological differences between Ronald Reagan (conservative), Richard Nixon (moderate), Pat Brown (liberal/reformist), and Jerry Brown (radical). Seen in this light, the differing formulations of social ethics within the evangelical community are highly predictable, as predictable as the clashing once was between Richard Nixon and Pat Brown. However, if evangelicals are to continue to be self-defined by their commitment to Biblical authority, their ongoing theological differences, though predictable, must be challenged. Evangelicals must be willing to work conscientiously toward a Biblically defined consensus regarding social ethics. Otherwise, a spade should be called a spade, and evangelicalism's Biblical position concerning authority should be modified.

An attempt at consensus-building regarding social ethics is one of contemporary evangelicalism's most critical tasks, but it will not prove an easy one to accomplish. For Scripture has within its pages "conservative," "moderate," "reformist," and "radical" thrusts. Its Biblical witness is not univocal. In framing a social ethic, it will always be, to some degree, a matter of interpreting, sifting, and choosing. Romans 13 (which sees government as God-ordained) and Revelation 13 (which sees government as demonic), exodus and captivity, the kingdom present and future, standards of equality and standards of need—all must be properly weighed. In this process, traditional interpretations can help, but they must not take on an exclusively authoritative status. If this is not to happen, or more accurately, perhaps, if this is not to continue, evangelicals need to recognize the problem and willingly engage in a therapeutic process of dialogue and joint formulation with fellow evangelicals from conflicting traditions. As Jim Wallis recognizes,

> Would it not be better to honestly identify the real differences of opinion among us and begin a more open and fruitful dialogue that might aid us all in discerning the shape of biblical politics?[53]

Or as Judy Brown Hull states:

> We should not be afraid to search out the extra-biblical authorities in our lives and to take the time with ourselves and with others to discover what else is operating to affect our "clear reading of the scriptures."[54]

1. What Do We Mean by Social Justice?

As evangelicals dialogue among themselves, they will discover that there is presently lacking in sections of their community a commitment to ground social ethics in a Biblically based understanding of "social justice." For example, of the four journals we have considered, only *The Reformed Journal* and *Sojourners* (those periodicals reflecting ethnic perspectives) commonly use the term. Too often, in that section of the evangelical community which stems from American revivalism and fundamentalism, discussion of social ethics passes over this foundational matter altogether, discussing instead only specific procedures. When "justice" is noted as the basis and goal of social ethics, it is all too often left undefined. More commonly, perhaps, when foundational matters are mentioned, they are reduced from "justice" to "compassion" alone.

Even David Moberg, for example (someone I have aligned with the perspective of *The Reformed Journal*), believes that the church's social task is best described using terms such as "social ministries, social obligations, social responsibility, social concern, social service, social welfare, or social action."[55] What is conspicuously absent, both in this quotation and in the rest of his book on social ethics, is the phrase "social justice." His is typical of the majority of evangelical discussion on the topic. Rather than centering on the goal of a Christian social ethic (i. e., justice), the evangelical church has settled traditionally for a debate over tactics (i. e., the proper action, service, ministry, or concern), or has reduced matters of ethics to humanitarian service.

In fairness to evangelicals, they are not alone in their difficulty with the concept of "social justice." The term "justice" has proven historically difficult to pin down. Jacques Ellul and Emil Brunner, to mention but two writers on the topic, consider the term undefinable.[56] Thus it is somewhat understandable, though hardly excusable, that evangelical Foy Valentine never bothered to specify what "justice" means, when he declared at the 1973 Thanksgiving Workshop on Evangelicals and Social Concern: "Justice. Nothing so upsets us as injustice. Is not this a universal phenomenon? . . . Justice simply has to be a major target for Christians concerned about social action." Valentine wrongly assumed, it seems, that the concept "justice" had a univocal meaning in society and in the church.[57]

In the absence of any concerted effort toward arriving at a univocal Biblically based definition of "justice," evangelicals have too often adopted certain working definitions from the American culture. These have been two in particular: "to each according to the person's merit or demerit" (the aristocratic) and "to each according to a standard of equality" (the democratic). Both definitions have limited usefulness, but both also are difficult to defend rationally or Biblically as the Christian's basic posture. Rationally, the aristocratic model suffers from the fact that it is justified only if each individual has an equal chance of achieving all the merit she or he is capable of. Competition being unequal, judgments based on its results are fallacious. Moreover, by what criterion is one to judge merit? Similarly, the democratic model proves inadequate. For whatever standard of arithmetical equality is selected (Aristotle chose "free birth"), it can be shown that such a norm exists only in a larger social context and thus participates in society's basic inequality. Such rational problems, however, are not the real issue for the evangelical church, important though they be. More serious for evangelicals is the fact that these two culturally derived models seem at odds with the Biblical witness concerning "social justice."

Rather than continue to use such culturally derived, and ultimately unsuccessful, definitions of "justice," the evangelical church must search out the Biblical norm. Here, the recent writings of the Reformed wing of evangelicalism, as well as those of "Anabaptist" writers, seem crucial. For a Biblical concept of justice has been the real concern of a few of these writers.[58] Evidence is of course mixed, but the overwhelming thrust of Scripture's discussion of "social justice" suggests the following Biblical definition: *"to each according to his or her needs."* Rather than act on the basis of society's most common definitions of "social justice"— those of merit or equality—the Christian seeking a Biblically derived social ethic must respond, first and foremost, on the basis of need. Such a judgment carries with it its own problems concerning definition, and it will be unacceptable on first reading to many within evangelicalism, for their traditions do not easily stretch to include such a notion as being that of "justice." At best this would seem a definition of "compassion," they would argue. But if the evidence from within Scripture is as strong as Biblical scholars are increasingly suggesting, evangelicals who wish to re-

main true to their self-defined norm of Biblical authority will need
to consider closely such a definition, regardless.

Evidence to back up this notion of justice ("to each according to
need") as Biblical comes from throughout Scripture. Although it is
not the Bible's purpose to give a careful scientific definition of what
our "needs" are, Scripture does repeatedly identify justice with assistance for the poor, the sick, and the powerless. Job states, for example:

> I put on righteousness [*sedaqah*], and it clothed me;
>   my justice [*mishpat*] was like a robe and a turban.
> I was eyes to the blind,
>   and feet to the lame.
> I was a father to the poor,
>   and I searched out the cause of him
>   whom I did not know.
> I broke the fangs of the unrighteous, and
>   made him drop his prey from his teeth.
>   [Job 29:14–17]

Paul understands justice along similar lines in his second letter to the
Corinthians:

> And God is able to provide you with every blessing in abun-
> dance, so that you may always have enough of everything and
> may provide in abundance for every good work. As it is writ-
> ten,
>
> > "He scatters abroad, he gives to the poor;
> > his righteousness [justice] endures for ever."
>
> He who supplies seed to the sower and bread for food will
> supply and multiply your resources and increase the harvest
> of your righteousness [justice].
>   [2 Cor. 9:8–10]

To buttress his point, Paul refers back to Psalm 112:9 where God's
righteousness, his justice *(sedaqah),* is defined in terms of his assistance to the poor (cf. Pss. 103:6; 146:7–9). Similarly, our righteousness, our justice *(dikaiosyne),* is to be seen in terms of the abundance
of our helpful deeds (our "every good work").

Such a concept of justice finds its full expression in the Christ-
event. In the Magnificat, Mary sings in praise of him who will reverse
the roles of the rich and the poor, the weak and the strong (Luke
1:46–53). Jesus similarly announces his mission as being that of releas-

ing the captives and preaching good news to the poor (Luke 4:18–19). Similarly, he judges his true followers to be those who practice a style of living based on the needs of the poor (Matt. 25:34–35). God's great act of salvation is for the poor and needy. And it is this that Paul labels an expression of God's righteousness *(dikaiosyne)*, i. e., justice (Rom. 1:16–17).

Support for such a notion of justice comes also from the Pentateuch where Israel's ancient laws (its sense of justice) protected the downtrodden and powerless, granting them special favor (Deut. 14: 28–29; Exod. 23:11). The prophets' indictment of Israel similarly centered on the fact that Israel had oppressed the poor and needy, ignoring the standards of justice which God had set up to protect these people (Zech. 7:9–10; Amos 5:7–15; Jer. 34:8–22).

Even where Scriptural evidence seems on first reading to contradict this bias toward the needy, closer inspection reveals that no real inconsistency exists. For example, the Law at times seems to set out as its standard a basic notion of equality. Leviticus 19:15 reads: " 'You shall do no injustice in judgment; you shall not be partial to the poor or defer to the great, but in righteousness shall you judge your neighbor.' " (See also Exod. 23:3; Deut. 25:1.) How does this correlate with "to each according to his or her need"? The answer lies in the basic difference between criminal (or retributive) justice and social (political and economic) justice. The needy are best protected by criminal justice being meted out impartially. Here is how God can best "judge . . . [his] people with righteousness, and . . . [his] poor with justice." (Ps. 72:2) But with regard to *social* justice, the God of the Bible reveals himself to have a distinct bias in favor of the poor and helpless (cf. Deut. 15:10; 1 Kings 1:53; Ps. 107:39–41). Jeremiah writes:

> "Did not your father eat and drink
> and do justice and righteousness?
> Then it was well with him.
> He judged the cause of the poor and needy;
> then it was well.
> Is this not to know me?
> says the LORD."
>
> [Jer. 22:15–16; cf. Deut. 10:12–22]

2. "Love" Versus "Justice"?

"To each according to each's needs" is a common *Christian* standard. Similarly, action on behalf of the poor and needy is widely praised by the church. But what is disputed among evangelicals, despite Biblical evidence such as that given above, is whether such an approach to social involvement is to be put under the rubric of "compassion" or of "justice." There is, in other words, a dichotomizing of love and justice which is widespread in evangelical circles.

Carl Henry, in an editorial in *Christianity Today,* has expressed succinctly and forcefully the dichotomous view of much of evangelicalism:

> Just as in his theological view of God the liberal dissolves righteousness into love, so in the political order he dilutes social justice into compassion. This kind of merger not only destroys the biblical view of God on the one hand but also produces the welfare state on the other. This confounding of justice and love confuses what God expects of government with what he expects of the Church, and makes the state an instrument for legislating partisan and sectarian ideals upon society. Ideally the purpose of the state is to preserve justice, not to implement benevolence.[59]

Mark Hatfield, in his book *Between a Rock and a Hard Place,* similarly distinguishes between love and justice. He discusses the conflict within him as a Christian between the "purist" and the "apologist." He understands the "purist" to base his action on self-giving love. The "apologist," on the other hand, knows that institutions cannot be based on such a principle and that simple justice must instead be the motive. Hatfield tries, he says, to remain a "purist," even in his role as senator, though the "apologist" continues necessarily to manifest himself.[60]

Reflecting still a third perspective within evangelicalism, David Moberg in the second part of his book *Inasmuch: Christian Social Responsibility in Twentieth Century America* spells out the Scriptural basis for Christian social concern. Moberg concludes: "God's will in the area of social concern can be summarized under the one instruction to *love.*" What is conspicuously absent in his Biblical analysis is any call to the achievement of social justice. The only two mentions of the word "justice" in this section, in fact, occur in discussions of the Old Testament prophets. And even here, justice is separated from and subordinated to love as being that which prevents love's denial.[61]

Fourth, arguing from an understanding of justice, Rus Walton states:

> Essential to the recognition of individual uniqueness is the recognition of the proper role of incentive and reward. He who works harder, and achieves more, and contributes more, is entitled to receive more. What he does with what he receives is up to him.[62]

Here again, the loving response and the just action are distinct, separable entities.

Thus, in representatives from the moderate, radical, reformist, and conservative camps within evangelicalism, we find a similar dichotomizing of love and justice. Henry and Walton understand justice as the primary referent for a Christian's participation in society, while Moberg and Hatfield stress love. There are problems, it seems to me, with either alternative. To stress love as one's motive for involvement encourages an overvaluation of voluntaristic structures as the key to Christian social ethics, and ultimately aborts rigorous structural involvement in society. Moreover, it permits societal positions of superiority and inferiority to remain intact. Too often, evangelicals have argued their understanding of social responsibility from the perspective of the "haves," rather than the "have-nots." An assumption of the point of view of benevolent power, rather than that of unjust powerlessness, seems almost the necessary outcome for even the most well-intentioned concentration on love.

To concentrate on justice (at least as understood by Henry) overcomes the problems listed above, but it creates its own tensions. To limit Christians to serving society's institutions from a perspective of justice forces their responses of love into the interstitial spaces. Although love will always find a form of expression, such a procedure reduces love to the extracurricular, as it were. But what person nurtured in the Bible can be content with such a radical restriction of love's context?[63]

What then is the solution? If evangelicals are to escape this present tension between the proper valuation of "love" on the one hand and "justice" on the other, they must listen more openly to one another. For both an emphasis on love and an emphasis on justice have their foundations Biblically. What must be recognized is that a Biblically based social ethic will be built on neither "justice" nor "love" as viewed in isolation, but instead on "loving justice." The Biblical writers do not understand social ethics in terms of one or the other of these human values, but in terms of the nature and activity of God who demonstrated their interconnectedness and indissolubility. God's justice (his righteousness) and his love (his mercy) are not clearly distinguished in Scripture and never separable in fact. Although these qualities are not identical, they "infect" one another (cf. Isa. 11:5; Jer. 9:24; Hos. 2:19). To understand God's righteousness, suggests Paul Ramsey, is to recognize that it has been invaded by the "vocabulary of salvation."[64]

The Old Testament, for example, does not contrast God's justice and his saving love, but rather posits that because he is a righteous God, therefore he is also a faithful and merciful savior (cf. Isa. 11: 3–4). Thus Hosea writes (Hos. 10:12):

> Sow for yourselves righteousness,
>   reap the fruit of steadfast love;
>   break up your fallow ground,
> for it is the time to seek the LORD,
>   that he may come and rain salvation upon you.

On the cross there is again this indistinguishable blending of God's justice and his love as God mercifully takes upon himself the just recompense due humanity. This loving center of God's righteousness is central to Paul's teaching about God, as Luther so forcefully discovered in meditating on Romans 1:16–17 (cf. Rom. 3:21–26). It is also central to a Biblical view of human justice. As with God, so his children are "to do justice, and to love kindness, and to walk humbly with . . . God." (Micah 6:8)

Seen in this light, the dichotomy of love versus justice must be countered as a sub-Christian notion and dismissed. In its place, a Biblically informed system of social ethics based in loving justice must be formulated. A dialogue between evangelicals committed to "love" as the basis for a social ethic and those committed to "justice" as its basis can only speed the day when this is recognized. For open dia-

logue will show that each position has Biblical support and value
while remaining incomplete as formulated. A recognition of the Biblical notion of "loving justice" as the basis for one's social ethic will
help evangelicals actualize their corporate responsibilities while filling
society's structures with a new humanity. It will also help them escape
their history of well-intentioned paternalism and meet their fellow
men and women as co-persons.

3. Are Human Beings Individual or Communal?

In a recent interview in *Sojourners*, Jim Wallis asked Carl Henry,
"Are there inherent things in particular formulations of evangelical
theology that are resistant to fundamental change in the social
order?"[65] In the paragraphs which follow, it becomes clear that behind
Wallis's question is his belief that traditional evangelical thought has
failed to deal with our fundamental human nature as social beings,
choosing instead to center on the solitary individual vis-à-vis God.
Ten years prior to Wallis's question, Lewis Smedes expressed a similar
concern in a response to Carl Henry's dialogue with Smedes in the
pages of *The Reformed Journal:*

> I have a notion that what separates Dr. Henry's thinking and
> mine is not so much a question of big or small government as
> such. . . . I think that where we differ, and where evangelicals
> ought to talk things out at length, is in the area of the doctrine
> of man and his community. I think we are not agreed on the
> subject of justice and rights among men because we have a
> significant shading of difference in our theology concerning
> man.[66]

Smedes goes on to characterize Henry's understanding of society's
basic component as being the individual, rather than the various social
spheres of family, church, and state.

The distinction that is being argued here is a complex one. Carl
Henry, for example, was able to respond to Jim Wallis's characteriza-
tion of the communal, over against the individual, nature of the gospel
by saying that he agreed with Wallis's communal definition.[67] But
Henry's individualistic view of *people* within human society, while
allowing for the community of the church, the importance of the
family, and a limited function for the state, remains largely atomistic.

It is this which explains many evangelicals' (including Henry's) basic apprehension concerning governmental involvement in economics and welfare. Most social involvement, Henry reasons, should be limited to the voluntary and/or contractual, being based in individual decision.

Such a commitment to individualism has a long history in the American evangelical church and has sometimes been overlooked by evangelicals in their discussions on involvement in the social arena. Timothy Smith's book *Revivalism and Social Reform in Mid-Nineteenth Century America,* for example, argues persuasively that nineteenth-century evangelicals with their quest for moral perfection were at the forefront of the social battle, fighting against poverty, slum housing, racial intolerance, and inhuman working conditions.[68] Smith's book has often been used by evangelicals to support their claim that they have been socially active. What is overlooked by Smith and his adherents in their discussion is the frontier-orientation of most of these nineteenth-century revivalists, i. e., their Jacksonian individualism. As the changing socio-economic conditions of nineteenth-century urban, industrial America demanded of the church a reassessment of its understanding of people in society, it was the Social Gospel movement which arose to take seriously the reality of corporate sin and the need for corporate response. Unfortunately, such a social definition of human nature proved unacceptable to the evangelical majority, and thus the Social Gospel became increasingly alienated from the conservative church, finding its theological resting-place in more liberal circles. It was in this way that the modernist-fundamentalist controversy was born, not first of all over matters of Scriptural interpretation, but over matters of social reality. The legacy of that debate is still ours.

What is necessary, today, if we are to overcome the hostility and theological accretions that have been built up within and outside evangelicalism, is a fresh assessment of the Biblical doctrine of humanity. And here, as before, the increasingly felt influence in evangelical circles of Calvinist and Anabaptist traditions can be significant. Having largely escaped because of the ethnic flavor of their communities the influence of American individualism, as well as much of the modernist-fundamentalist acrimony, these segments (represented in our discussion by *The Reformed Journal* and by *Sojourners*) can lead the wider evangelical church back to a Biblical understanding of man/woman.

As they do, humanity's corporate nature will emerge. "Male and female created he them," states the writer of Genesis 1:27 (KJV). Here is the meaning of the image of God: relationship, co-humanity. Similarly, when Yahweh graciously covenanted, it was not with isolated souls but with a people. Again, Jesus incorporates those whom he saves into his body. And so the Biblical witness goes. Viewing the Biblical materials through an interpretive grid based in the individualism and voluntarism of American life, many evangelicals have been forced both to ignore the corporate witness of the Old Testament and to isolate certain individualistic thrusts within the New. An adequate evangelical social ethic will need to once again listen to the Biblical sources in their entirety regarding the nature of human beings.

4. How Should the Church Be Involved Politically?

In the preceding discussion, I have often grouped together the editorial positions of *Sojourners* and *The Reformed Journal.* But there is an important difference between these two viewpoints in evangelicalism which now must be explored. The issue is that of political strategy, and the right use of power to achieve it. What is the true shape of Biblical politics?

In an editorial entitled "What Does Washington [i. e., *Sojourners*] Have to Say to Grand Rapids [i. e., *The Reformed Journal*]?" *Sojourners* editor Jim Wallis characterized the disagreement from his perspective:

> A rather persistent pattern of criticism has emerged against *Sojourners* from a group of people suggesting that our commitment to the building of community signals a withdrawal from the world, that we are more concerned with an "alternative lifestyle" than with social justice, and that we are apolitical, or not political enough, or at least not political in the right ways.[69]

Wallis disputes the charge of political irresponsibility by saying that he understands political involvement in different terms from his Reformed colleagues. A Biblical vision of social ethics must involve social, political, and economic realities to be sure. But these realities, for Wallis, must be viewed as standing under the judgment of an ethic of the kingdom. What this means concretely is that Christians must engage themselves in effective political critique on the one hand and in an alternate, community-based involvement with the poor on the other.

The church exists as a sojourner, an alien in a strange and godless land. Its political strategy must, therefore, take on the form of dissent and resistance; it must stand over against the prevalent structures and values of society. States Wallis, "The church of Jesus Christ is at war with the systems of the world, not détente, ceasefire, or peaceful coexistence, but at war."[70] Acting on this belief, Wallis led his *Sojourners* community in over forty public actions during the first six months of 1977, protesting such issues as the use of torture, the proliferation of nuclear armaments, and the government's repressive housing policies. Second, the church must also be, in Wallis's words, a "sort of pilot project of a whole new order of things."[71] It must create a new community as an alternative power structure, a local community whose common life is characterized by service to the needy and radical obedience to the Lordship of Jesus Christ. The Christian's life is political in that it is to create a counter-community which is more conducive to human life, justice, and freedom than those structures presently existing. Here, then, is one form of evangelical political understanding—one reminiscent of earlier Anabaptist thought, emphasizing political critique and alternate communal modeling.

Such a political program has been opposed by those evangelicals of the Reformed tradition, because "for all of its political relevance and all of its political language, it is in the end an apolitical strategy rejecting power, and thus rejecting politics as well."[72] While political critique and communal activity are advocated which have political consequences, any direct political involvement is shunned. For as Wes Michaelson states:

> when you get involved in the political order, you then are asked continually to compromise, relegate, reinterpret, or dismiss central New Testament teachings in order to preserve your own place within the order, or to preserve the government itself on the terms which it defines. To gain power within

the system, I have to play according to its rules which are part of a fallen order, directly in contradiction to the kingdom that I have given my life to.[73]

Those in the Reformed tradition see in Michaelson's apoliticalness an underlying fatalism that both denies the power of the risen Lord over all creation and undercuts love's effectiveness in action. In Christ, God is working for the renewal of his creation. Thus, if Christians are to imitate Christ (a favorite theme of *Sojourners*), they must carry forward that work of renewal in all spheres of life, including the political arena, even while recognizing the partial, imperfect nature of their efforts. While the positive results of past efforts have been limited, they have nevertheless been real. Christian activity has been responsible for introducing new concepts of social responsibility, while at the same time alleviating some of the suffering, injustice, and oppression caused by society. *The Reformed Journal* editor Nicholas Wolterstorff argues that as a Christian

> One must engage in ameliorative politics, and to do so one must calculate what would bring success. How can one seriously preach judgment to the oppressors and not do what one can to relieve the oppressed? The fact that the politics of earth is not the harmony of heaven renders neither irrelevant nor illegitimate our engagement in that politics.[74]

Fundamental to this difference between *Sojourners* and *The Reformed Journal* over political involvement and strategy is a conflicting understanding of hermeneutics. And it is here, perhaps, that constructive theological dialogue can begin. For Wallis's ultimate rejection of a *Realpolitik* (working within the corrupt "political" system to effectively garner power for human ends) is based on his understanding of Jesus' *servanthood* (identifying with the poor and oppressed, but rejecting all solutions based on political power). But will such a hermeneutical approach to Scripture hold up under close scrutiny? Because Jesus did not fight Rome, for example, should the confessing Christians in Germany in World War II have remained nonpolitical as well? Surely not. As Wolterstorff recognizes, "the fact that Jesus never ran for political office does not become an objection to running for political office, any more than the fact that he never heard a piano concerto becomes an objection to listening to piano concertos."[75]

For those in the Reformed tradition, it is not a literalistic *imitatio Christi,* but a recognition of the ongoing validity of a doctrine of creation that provides the basis for a Christian social ethic. Christ's resurrection allows his people to view all of creation not from the perspective of its victims alone, but also from the viewpoint of Christ's victory. A belief in the renewal of the world is not the same as a commitment to a superficial doctrine of progress. The latter is based on human achievement, and flounders because of it. The former is based on God's activity, and finds both a certainty for its hope in the proleptic event of the resurrection and an ongoing witness in the Spirit's activity in the world.

5. Evangelism Versus Social Justice?

In the editorial positions described above there was a widespread recognition that both evangelism and social action are necessary. But the priorities assigned to each of these aspects of Christian mission differed markedly. There was the *"conservative"* position which declared that evangelism—the conversion of individuals to Christ—was primary, though Christians should also be compassionate in their social action. Here, evangelism was seen as the Christian's priority task, as well as the inevitable first step toward social concern. The *"moderates"* recognized that evangelism without the parallel call to discipleship was sub-Christian and an invitation to "cheap grace." Thus evangelism—the announcement that Christ forgives and recreates—should be put within the context of a costly obedience. The Great Commission and The Great Commandment belong together. However, as Billy Graham stated at Lausanne's International Congress on World Evangelization, while efforts at social justice are important, they are "not our priority mission."[76]

The *"reformists"* altered the position of social action from that of a subset of, or consequence of, evangelism to that of an equal partner with evangelism in the mission task of the church. The conversion of individuals through the proclamation of the good news and the political restructuring of society for the sake of greater social justice through Christian social action are joint priorities for the

Christian. Finally, the *"radical"* evangelical position is suspicious of socio-political liberation as the task of the church, but mindful that the good news is corporate and addressed to the whole person. Thus, the primary mission of the church is the proclamation and building up of the church, that new society based in the kingdom of God where an alternate personal, economic, social, and spiritual life-style can be modeled. As John Yoder states, "the very existence of the church is her primary task."[77]

While not downplaying the importance of personal regeneration, the need for radical discipleship, or the call to the building-up of the church, I believe such emphases tend to obfuscate a genuine, Biblically centered social ethic. Only as the commitment to social justice is given "separate, but equal" status can it operate creatively in its full integrity. Such a concern that social justice receive equal billing in the church's missionary task is motivated by two factors—the Biblical and the pragmatic. On Biblical grounds, we note, for example, that Jesus' ministry is summarized in the Gospels in ways like the following: "And he went about all Galilee, teaching in their synagogues, and preaching the gospel of the kingdom *and* healing every disease and every infirmity among the people." (Matt. 4:23, my italics) (See also Matt. 9:35; 11:1–6; Luke 4:18–19.) Jesus' ministry included preaching and healing; it was a ministry to the whole person. Pragmatically, we must conclude that societal reconstruction based on a missionary agenda of evangelism and/or discipleship has never worked. Nor has the Anabaptist emphasis on the reconstruction of the church been effective in changing society. If, as Samuel Escobar claimed at Lausanne, "concern for the integrity of the Gospel . . . motivates us to stress its social dimension," then social action must be understood as standing alongside evangelism if the church's agenda for mission is to be effectively enacted.[78]

Increasingly, such a concern for the salvation of the whole person *is* being voiced in evangelicalism. Richard Quebedeaux, in his book *The Young Evangelicals,* discusses the fact at some length, finding that certain campus-oriented ministries (Inter-Varsity Christian Fellowship and the Christian World Liberation Front) are particularly sensitive to the issue.[79] Samuel Escobar, connected with the student population through his work in Latin America with the International Fellowship of Evangelical Students, perhaps provides the reason:

Many young people in Latin America, who were motivated by the Gospel to love their neighbor and be concerned for justice and freedom in their society, have often become Marxists simply because their churches did not provide biblical instruction about Christian discipleship, or because they [their churches] were blind to clear demands from the Bible and opportunities and challenges provided by new social situations.[80]

It is a partial failure in the task of evangelism and discipleship that has proved the catalyst for a reappraisal of campus-oriented mission. In the process some campus-related evangelicals have made a contribution to the entire church, helping to once again direct Christian mission along its two interrelated, but separate paths.

Conclusion

Evangelism and social justice, political power and the power of servanthood, the individual and the community, love and justice, these are the polarities that the evangelical church must address as it moves toward a Biblically informed consensus regarding social ethics. Evidence from the conflicting theological heritages of evangelicals can be rallied to support both sides of each pairing. But basic to each of these issues will be evangelicalism's ability to agree on a definition of "social justice" itself. What, therefore, is involved in this discussion is not merely the issue of ethics, but also of hermeneutics. How are the Biblical texts to be read, so as to allow Scripture to act authoritatively in the church's life and practice? This chapter has suggested an approach for answering that question, finding in the dialogue between competing traditions a resource for Biblical reanalysis.

Using such an approach, I have attempted to spell out the direction such a Biblically defined interpretation of social ethics might take. The Biblical record seems to indicate equal billing for evangelism and for efforts at social justice. If efforts at social justice are to be effective, we cannot shy away from political involvement in the structures of society. If the individual is perhaps the focus for efforts in evangelism, the person as communal is the rightful focus of the church's social ethic. While love and justice are separable concepts in theory, in fact they are made inseparable for the Christian by their mutuality and indissolubility in God's self-revelation. Although "equality" is certainly an important standard of retributive justice that Scripture holds up, an inspection of the Biblical text reveals that "need" is the true locus of God's notion of social justice.

Whether such an analysis as the one I have offered harbingers the direction an evangelical consensus will take depends ultimately on its faithfulness to the Biblical record. It also depends on the willingness of those within the evangelical church to reassess and reinterpret their cherished ethical positions in dialogue with fellow evangelicals whose differing theological traditions push them in new directions. Given evangelicalism's common loyalty to Jesus Christ as Lord and to Scripture as authoritative, such reevaluation is possible. The agenda is set; evangelicals must now begin the task of dialogue and consensus-building.

V

Homosexuality and the Evangelical: The Influence of Contemporary Culture

In its first issue for the year 1978, *Christianity Today* asked a variety of evangelical leaders to assess what was the most noteworthy religious development of the previous year and to predict what would be most important in the upcoming one. Hudson Armerding, president of Wheaton College responded, "I personally feel that the issue of homosexuals in the church was one of the most significant religious developments of the year." Stephen Board, editor of *Eternity* magazine, replied, "In 1978 I think that the most interesting story will be the response of the United Presbyterian Church to various conservative concerns, specifically the question of the ordination of homosexuals." Russell Chandler, evangelical religion writer for the *Los Angeles Times,* concurred and added, "Division among many Christians about how far to go in accepting—if not embracing—homosexuals will dominate religious news for several years."[1]

Homosexuality and the Church

Although the issue of homosexuality is only now surfacing as a major area of theological controversy for evangelicals, it erupted as early as 1972 among mainline Protestant churches in America. In that year, William Johnson, a self-declared homosexual, was ordained for the ministry by the United Church of Christ. In 1972, as well, *Motive,* the United Methodist Church's youth publication, stopped production amid controversy, publishing as its final volume two simultaneous issues advocating a gay life-style.[2] In 1973, *Trends,* a publication of the United Presbyterian Church, devoted a full issue to the topic "Homosexuality: Neither Sin Nor Sickness."[3] Also in 1973, an ecumenical National Task Force on Gay People in the Church was recognized by the governing board of the National Council of Churches.

Since then, interest in the subject of homosexuality and the church has mushroomed to the point that there are presently fourteen denominational gay caucuses seeking acceptance for homosexuals in the church. Denomination-wide task forces or committees have responded by drafting (or are in the process of drafting) study documents on homosexuality for the United Church of Christ (U.C.C.), the United Presbyterian Church (U.P.C.), the Presbyterian Church, U.S. (P.C.U.S.), the Episcopal Church (whose Bishop of New York ordained as a deacon in 1975 a self-declared lesbian, Ellen Barrett), and the American Lutheran Church (A.L.C.). Moreover, these studies are not uniformly finding homosexuality to be sinful. The P.C.U.S. report, for example, concludes that "in view of the complexity of the issue, the disagreement among Christians and the variety in the character and experience of homosexual persons themselves, it seems unwise at this time to propose any one position as *the* position of our Church."[4] The U.P.C. task-force majority report, which was ultimately rejected at the General Assembly level, was even less traditional. For in granting local congregations and presbyteries the option of ordaining self-affirmed sexually active homosexuals, it seemed to indicate that homosexuality *per se* was not to be considered sinful.

Books on the church and homosexuality have been rolling off secular and church presses alike in increasing numbers.[5] These books present a wide range of theological positions, from condemning homosexuality as a particularly vile sin to advocating it as an alternative approach to loving relationships. Outside of the traditional denominational structures, but seeking affirmation by established churches, the Metropolitan Community Church (M.C.C.) has ministered primarily to gay Christians since its inception in 1968. It reported at the end of 1976 a total membership of 20,731 in 103 congregations. Taken together, such evidence suggests that homosexuality has become a major theological concern of the Protestant church in America.

In spite of the general interest in the topic among the wider Protestant church, it is surprising that homosexuality has become a major issue among evangelicals. For evangelicals have traditionally held the Bible to be clear on this point. Richard Lovelace represents the past evangelical consensus when he argues: "If we can reinterpret the Scripture to endorse homosexual acts among Christians, we can make it endorse anything else we want to do or believe."[6] Such would have been the near-unanimous opinion of evangelical theologians until recently. And such remains the opinion of an overwhelming number of evangelical lay women and men. *The Christian Herald*, for example, polled its readers in January of 1978 and found that 94% opposed the ordination of homosexuals, even if otherwise qualified.[7] A survey of 60,000 *McCall's* readers produced a similar result; 70% of those labeling themselves born-again Christians considered homosexuality to be "sinful, unethical or immoral."[8] Yet an increasing, albeit small, number of evangelicals are suggesting that the church's theological position regarding homosexuality must be rethought. Such a suggestion has brought an immediate and varied response from the evangelical press, as the recent output concerning homosexuality in evangelical periodicals attests. *His, The Wittenburg Door, The Journal of the American Scientific Affiliation, Eternity, Daughters of Sarah, The Reformed Journal, Christianity Today, Inspiration, Moody Monthly, The Christian Herald, Faith at Work, The Other Side*—all have had since 1977 major features or whole issues devoted to a Christian understanding of homosexuality.[9]

The topic of homosexuality is being pushed to the theological forefront in evangelical circles for a specific reason. While conflict between Reformed, Anabaptist, and American fundamentalist traditions has been largely responsible, as we have seen, for fostering division over the church's understanding of social ethics, and while a lack of consensus regarding Biblical hermeneutics lies behind much of the continuing controversy concerning women's place in marriage and church, it is the influence of contemporary culture that has forced evangelicals to reconsider their theological understanding of homosexuality. Moreover, it is in conflicting views concerning the theological usefulness of contemporary culture that one can discern the developing lines of division within evangelicalism concerning homosexuality in the church.

The Role of Contemporary Culture

The gay liberation movement was born on a summer evening in 1969 in New York's Greenwich Village when patrons at the Stonewall Inn, a gay bar, resisted police harassment. The resulting riot lasted three nights and "gay power" was a reality. Since then gays have accomplished much. Presently it is estimated that there are over 1,800 gay organizations. Gays have lobbied successfully to get homosexuality both decriminalized and demedicalized. In 1973 the American Bar Association called on state legislatures to repeal all laws which place homosexual activity between consenting adults in private in the category of a *crime*. In 1973, as well, the American Psychiatric Association voted to remove homosexuality from the category of *illnesses* and the American Psychological Association similarly voted to remove homosexuality from the category of the *abnormal*. What gay advocates have also sought is to persuade the church to remove homosexuality from the category of *sin*. The church is no longer able to remain neutral; it must respond affirmatively or negatively.

Besides the pressure of public demands, the personal testimony of increasingly bold homosexual Christians within the church is forcing evangelicals to rethink their position. At a leading evangelical church in New York City, for example, after the morning worship service one of the outstanding elders stood and announced to a hushed congregation that he could no longer hide from them his homosexuality. He asked for their affirmation of himself as he was, homosexuality and all. The Presbyterian Task Force to Study Homosexuality had as one of its members Chris Glaser, a self-avowed gay Christian. Discussion becomes in such a situation radically concrete. Gay Christians are claiming that they are "the *best* source" for the church as it attempts to understand the homosexual.[10] As U.C.C. minister William Johnson writes:

> Rather than looking to the psychologists and the psychiatrists and the sociologists, and even to the theologians, to find out about gay people, there is a need to listen to gay people within

our churches and within the society, to begin to understand what *we* perceive to be the problems, and then together to work on those problems.[11]

What gay Christians perceive is widespread homophobia (revulsion and/or fear of homosexuality) in the church which has kept it from formulating an adequate theological response. Evangelicals must respond to the charge.

Finally, culture is pressuring the church regarding its traditional theology of homosexuality by providing it with new data from the social sciences. Perhaps the single most significant event in bringing on the current dislocation in evangelical churches was the publishing of the Kinsey Report in 1948. What Kinsey suggested, and what subsequent work by Masters and Johnson, Evelyn Hooker, and Paul Gebhard has confirmed, is that the incidence of homosexuality in America is higher than most church members imagined. Rather than homosexual activity being confined to a few people who are abnormal, Kinsey documented the fact that it must be viewed much more widely on a continuum of human sexuality that runs from the exclusively heterosexual to the exclusively homosexual. Kinsey indicated that on this continuum, at least 37% of the male population and 12% of the female population had some kind of overt homosexual experience between adolescence and old age. Those who were exclusively homosexual throughout their lifetime were 4% of the adult male population and 1 to 2% of the adult female. In terms of numbers those percentages translate into contemporary society as 4.5 million Americans. Paul Gebhard, the current director of Indiana University's Institute for Sex Research, has recently indicated that that figure might actually be as high as 5.8 million. He concludes, "Considering problems of sampling, etc. I would prefer to think the true number [of predominant or exclusive homosexuals] at any one time lies between 4 and 6 million."[12] Whatever the precise number, by the time you include parents, brothers, and sisters, such a statistic suggests that homosexuality is of central concern to a large percentage of the American people. These people are looking to the church to see how it will respond to them.

Almost every recent article or book by evangelicals begins, not with Scripture, but with cultural data from societal events, personal experience, or scientific analysis.[13] Although some evangelicals attempt to dismiss such input (e. g., Anita Bryant in her interview in *Playboy* refused to accept Kinsey's statistics for "he had no spiritual beliefs, no religious beliefs"[14]), most have admitted the need for greater knowledge and have sought out information from the larger culture. What they have discovered is that there exists a great variety among homosexuals; they can't be stereotyped. Not all male homosexuals are effeminate, nor do all lesbians hate men. Some are trouble-prone and sex-obsessed, but others lead well-adjusted, quiet lives. In an exhaustive study of 1,500 homosexuals in the San Francisco area by psychologist Alan Bell and sociologist Martin Weinberg entitled *Homosexualities: A Study of Diversity Among Men & Women,* the homosexuals' life-style is documented as ranging from "closed couples" to "open couples," "functionals" to "dysfunctionals" and "asexuals."[15] Perhaps all that homosexuals have in common is their defining characteristic: the propensity to be sexually aroused by thinking of or seeing or physically contacting persons of the same gender.

Having noted the strong influence of contemporary knowledge and experience on the issue, it is not surprising that the current lack of scientific agreement on this topic is the single most important source of present evangelical conflict. The larger culture has both raised the issue of homosexuality for the church and left in doubt several crucial judgments concerning its nature. Surely the central unresolved question is whether homosexuality is to be considered normal or abnormal. Although the American Psychiatric Association and the American Psychological Association voted in 1973 to "demedicinize" homosexuality, a recent poll of 2,500 psychiatrists revealed that 69% continue to think that homosexuality is a pathological adaptation (as opposed to a normal variation), while 13% expressed uncertainty and only 18% dissented.[16]

The judgment on whether or not homosexuality is a pathology will affect one's conclusions concerning both the cause (etiology) of homosexuality and its remedy. If homosexuality is a normal variation of human sexuality, the motivation to uncover its real cause is lessened and the topic of cure is made superfluous. If it is a sickness or an abnormality, its cause(s) and cure(s) become central. But here again, unfortunately, scientific data are conflicting and incomplete. Some posit as homosexuality's source an arrested state of development; others, an inadequate family structure. Some feel the absence of opposite-sex targets in early puberty holds the key; others, that the competitive and aggressive male ideal in American life has been eroti-cized and then possessed sexually. The evidence to date does not permit any definitive statements as to cause. Ralph Blair concludes his survey of the etiological literature by saying: "The theories are contra-dictory, incomplete, and based on inadequate samples of patients examined and interpreted by clinicians from different schools of thought without the control of standard definitions and procedures."[17] Yet most theorists concur that homosexuality is a learned behavior; " 'the process takes place primarily after birth and the basic funda-mentals are completed before puberty.' "[18]

As evangelicals make use of such scientific opinion as to the cause(s) of homosexuality, they are finding themselves to differ over the emphasis which should be placed on the fact it is a *learned* response, rather than an involuntary *patterning* from an early age which precludes choice. If one's homosexual orientation is pro-grammed through a kind of patterning, then responsibility is thought by some to be lacking and acceptance of the homosexual's orientation as a given would seem both a realistic and a "moral" approach to homosexuality. Instead of seeking to cure homosexuals, the Christian might instead seek to help homosexuals live more self-actualizing lives as they are (that is, if the Biblical data can be reevaluated). If homo-sexuality's *learned* nature is made the focus, then it would seem likely that one should be able to unlearn it with the help of psychological and/or spiritual aids. If so, the evangelical church must proclaim the power of God to cure homosexuals from their sinful orientation. The possibility, or lack thereof, of a "cure" for homosexuality is in this way becoming central to the developing debate among evangelicals. We will need to look in some detail at the arguments in what follows.

Medical opinion toward the homosexual remains an unsettled issue within contemporary debate. What is clear, however, is that homosexuality involves both one's orientation and one's expression of that orientation—there are both motivational and behavioral factors. A homosexual person is not, first of all, one who engages in given physical, sexual acts, or even one with certain feelings, wishes, and fantasies toward someone of the same sex, but one with a propensity for such activities and/or feelings. The awareness that homosexuality is first of all a "condition," or "orientation," and only secondarily one's thoughts and actions does not seem to have been recognized prior to the turn of the century. If this is indeed the case, then certainly this distinction was foreign to the Biblical writers. What, if anything, this implies concerning a Christian response to homosexuality is again disputed. Here as well, contemporary judgments are the occasion for the rising evangelical debate.

Thus, a brief survey of current discussion concerning homosexuality already suggests major divergencies which evangelical theologians are taking. Homosexuality can, for this reason, serve as a test case for evangelical theology in how to make use of contemporary culture (whether it is social pressure, scientific analysis, or personal testimony). Should the contemporary homosexual challenge be the occasion for a redefinition of the traditional view of both human sexuality and homosexuality? How does the Bible as final arbiter relate to the possibility of new insights or corrective thrusts from God through his creation? The issue once again is the question of theological hermeneutics, or interpretation. Can the Bible truly function as the ultimate rule of faith and practice amid theological ferment currently motivated by cultural influences? If so, how?

Current Evangelical Assessments

In his article "Homosexuality and the Church," James B. Nelson offers "a typology of four possible theological stances toward homosexuality."[19] Nelson uses as his examples well-known theologians who, for the most part, stand outside the evangelical tradition. At the most negative pole for Nelson are those holding to a *"rejecting-punitive"* approach—one which "unconditionally rejects homosexuality as legitimate and bears a punitive attitude toward homosexual persons." Nelson believes there are no major contemporary theologians who take this position. This stance, however, is amply attested to in the life of the church. A second position he labels the *"rejecting-nonpunitive"* stance. Swiss theologian Karl Barth adopted this approach, arguing that although men and women come into full humanity only in relation with persons of the opposite sex, God's grace precludes any condemnation of the homosexual *person* even while the sinfulness of homosexuality is maintained.

A third theological option mentioned by Nelson is that of homosexuality's *"qualified acceptance."* Theologians like the German Helmut Thielicke are arguing that although homosexuality is a "perversion" of the created order, its "constitutional" nature is not always susceptible of either treatment or sublimation. In such cases, homosexuals must seek the optimal ethical possibility (adult, faithfully committed relationships). The fourth theological stance is that of the *"full acceptance"* of homosexuality as a natural variation of human sexuality. English theologian Norman Pittenger takes such a tack, arguing that loving same-sex relationships are fully capable of expressing God's humanizing intentions.

What is interesting for our purposes is that this typology of theological options for the church holds true not only in those wider ecumenical circles where pluralistic approaches to theological authority are taken, but also within the evangelical community which seeks to distinguish itself by an allegiance to the Bible as its final arbiter. Nelson's categorization of the theological discussion concerning homosexuality is proving equally valid for the developing evangelical debate. As in the larger Christian community, no major evangelical theologian holds to a *punitive* approach, though it is observable in the evangelical popular press. Richard Lovelace and Don Williams, both evangelical members of the United Presbyterian Task Force on Homosexuality, represent variations of the *rejecting nonpunitive* position. Reformed theologian Lewis Smedes and Lutheran theologian Helmut Thielicke illustrate those evangelicals who are arguing for homosexuality's *qualified acceptance.* And coauthors Letha Scanzoni and Virginia Mollenkott and evangelical psychotherapist Ralph Blair argue with differing degrees of certitude for the *full acceptance* of loving, committed homosexual relations. Let me describe more fully how this range of opinion is developing.

1. A Rejecting-Punitive Approach

Both the success and the excess of Anita Bryant's Dade County, Florida campaign have focused the prevalent Christian bigotry that persists concerning homosexuality. For example, Jerry Falwell, the successful evangelical television minister, introduced Bryant at one rally by saying that the " 'So-called gay folks [would] just as soon kill you as look at you.' "[20] Popular evangelist Jack Wyrtzen is quoted in a similar vein, exclaiming to a different anti-gay-rights rally: " 'Homosexuality is a sin so rotten, so low, so dirty, that even cats and dogs don't practice it.' "[21] Gay evangelical Ralph Blair has had evangelical leaders describe homosexuality to him as a " 'vile, filthy, wicked, ungodly, low-down, beastly, degenerate, horrible sin,' " and Anita Bryant makes much the same assessment in her *Playboy* interview.[22] Such hysteria must be challenged. The widespread prejudice against homosexuals which now exists in the evangelical community under the guise of righteous indignation must end. Even if the evangelical church reaffirms as its consensus the sinful nature of homosexuality (whether orientation or activity or both) it cannot deny the gospel's central thrust by seeking punitive measures toward homosexuals. A Victorian backlash against the gay movement finds no theological support.

2. A Rejecting-Nonpunitive Stance

Representative of those books resisting the trend toward the ordination of avowed and practicing homosexuals are two volumes by Richard Lovelace and Don Williams. Lovelace's book, *The Church and Homosexuality* (1978), calls the church to defend itself through the dynamics of the spiritual life against the neopaganism of gay advocates who are presently challenging it. The church must not endorse their views or change its position, but Lovelace believes it must be willing to listen, study, and respond.

For Lovelace, the first step in this study process is an examination of the church's own received teachings. Summarizing the writings of Augustine, Aquinas, Luther, Calvin, Barth, and Thielicke, Lovelace finds the traditional theological interpretation to be that homosexuality is a sin, perhaps as Calvin wrote, " 'the most serious of all' " sins.[23] Second, Lovelace surveys the new theological approaches to homosexuality which have surfaced in response to society's reevaluation. Beginning with Bailey's *Homosexuality and the Western Christian Tradition* (1955), he notes the major theological commentators on the subject up to and including Scanzoni and Mollenkott's *Is the Homo-sexual My Neighbor?* (1978). Lovelace evaluates the current theologi-cal direction, concluding that one can detect in the growing accept-ance of homosexuality a "false religion" (its antipathy toward Biblical revelation is a sign), a "cheap grace" (repentance is ignored), a "power-less grace" (the possibility of cure is denied), and an "antinomian ethic" (the balance between Law and gospel is undercut).

Only after completing his theological assessment does Lovelace turn to the Biblical evidence for support of his position. He finds five texts (Lev. 18:22; 20:13; Rom. 1:26–27; 1 Cor. 6:9, 10; 1 Tim. 1:8–11) which teach that "homosexual behavior is contrary to the will of God."[24] Tellingly, Lovelace turns to texts teaching on human sexual-ity more generally, only after he has considered the specific passages prohibiting homosexual practice. Moreover, he finds general sexual expression to be grounded in the covenant of heterosexual marriage, not in the prior creation of human beings as male and female. This leads Lovelace to assert:

> Fornication, adultery, and homosexual practice are not simply itemized as forbidden behavior; they are treated as objects of shame and loathing. It even seems that biblically there are legitimate forms of "homophobia" and "heterophobia" so long as the fear and hatred implied by these words are focused on *behavior* and not on *persons.*[25]

What is the church's ministry to homosexuals? The church, Love-lace feels, must undertake a dual repentance—"gay" Christians must renounce their active life-style and "straight" Christians, their homo-phobia. Beyond this the church should sponsor the ministries of avowed, but repentant, homosexuals within the gay communities and call homosexuals to be cured through the dynamics of the spiritual life. Conspicuously absent in Lovelace's discussion is any wrestling with the data of the empirical sciences. Such, he feels, are not directly useful as a source of ethical norms, being at best value-free, or more typically, anti-Christianly biased. Though culture can call the church to reevaluate its theology, Lovelace believes it has little, if anything, constructive to contribute to the theological task once begun.

Don Williams's book *The Bond That Breaks: Will Homosexuality Split the Church?* (1978) uses a radically different methodology from that of Lovelace. After relating his personal experience with homosexuals in counseling and after analyzing the contemporary movement toward gay liberation, Williams devotes successive chapters to a discussion of four social scientists' views of homosexuality, to an analysis of the Biblical teaching, and finally to a presentation of the positions of three representative theologians—Barth (traditional), Thielicke (moderating), and McNeill (accepting).

Williams concludes his survey of contemporary theological trends concerning homosexuality by noting "the growing weight which is given to the 'facts' proposed by the social scientists on the nature of homosexuality."[26] Yet the variety of theories and definitions stemming from the observation of the homosexual phenomena suggests to Williams that such "facts" must be judged according to an outside authoritative standard. This Williams finds in the Biblical position. But even if the social sciences were more unanimous, Williams would want the Bible—"God's revelation of his will"—to be the starting point. He concludes:

> We can never depend on observation leading us to divine order. Rather, we must let the revelation of God guide us in our observation of the world around us.
>
> When the social sciences have the first word, the Bible may have the second word, but the social sciences will be the final arbiter as they select what of the Bible is relevant for us.[27]

Thus, where historical theology guides Lovelace (who is a church historian at Gordon-Conwell Seminary), Biblical theology is the starting point for Williams (who is a New Testament scholar at Claremont Men's College).

Where Lovelace comes to the Bible seeking specific passages to buttress traditional theological viewpoints, Williams comes to the Bible seeking guidance in the conflicting discussion of the empirical sciences. He finds in the opening chapters of Genesis such a perspective. For not only are these foundational for all Christian theology, but they reveal specifically God's order for human sexuality. God has created persons "to live as male and female before Him and with each other. This order determines our proper sexual relationship."[28] It is in the creation of humanity itself, and not in God's subsequent blessing on the covenant of marriage, that Williams finds the definitive Biblical word regarding homosexuality. Humanity is created male *or* female to live as male *and* female (Barth). "Having understood Genesis 1—3, the rest of the Bible falls into place," asserts Williams.[29] Sodom (Gen. 19) and Gibeah (Judg. 19) become illustrations of the violent challenge to God's order for human sexuality. The Levitical laws reflect this same ordering in their condemnation of male homosexual acts, as does 1 Timothy 1:10 whose catalogue of sins is a reworking of the Decalogue. Jesus' teaching (e. g., Matt. 19) and Paul's letters (e. g., Rom. 1) affirm the order of creation.

Williams understands the opening chapters of Genesis as revealing three divine gifts to humanity: order, purpose, and freedom. God graciously *orders* us male or female, creating cosmos from chaos. Moreover, he calls us to fulfill his *purpose* by reflecting his image by living together in *freedom* as male and female. Homosexuality as an abuse of this freedom, a denial of humanity's purpose, and a flouting of the divine order has its origins in the fall itself. It is not a "special" sin as some think, but it nevertheless is a sin. Repentance and restoration to the divine image in Christ are called for.

3. Qualified Acceptance

Lovelace and Williams choose to focus their theological analysis, not in personal testimony or empirical evidence, but in church history (Lovelace) and Biblical theology (Williams). The emphasis of those who are arguing for a "qualified acceptance" of homosexuals tends in a different direction. Such writers as Helmut Thielicke and Lewis Smedes seek to deal *concretely* and *pastorally* with the tragedy of "an ethically upright, mature homosexual who is struggling with his condition."[30] Though tradition and Biblical theology inform their judgments, Thielicke and Smedes find contemporary observers (both homosexuals themselves and social scientists) to be necessary and equal partners in the process of theological formation. For both Williams and Lovelace, the evidence of contemporary culture is to be considered secondarily, if at all, as a general theological statement concerning homosexuality is hammered out. For Thielicke and Smedes, on the other hand, the evidence from contemporary culture is thought to be crucial and is given an equal footing with that of

Biblical exegesis and historical theology, as pastoral counsel is given to real people with real suffering.

Two concrete matters are given particular weight by Thielicke and Smedes in their analyses: first, that there are occasional, stable, loving homosexual relationships; and second, that a generally effective therapy or cure, whether in the clinic or the church, is lacking. If it is true that homosexuality is at times "incurable" and that stable monogamous homosexual relationships are possible, even if difficult, could it be that homosexual practice might be counseled as the optimal ethical possibility in some cases? Both Thielicke and Smedes raise the suggestion tentatively as a possible position for the pastoral counselor.

Along with G. C. Berkouwer, Helmut Thielicke is the most influential Continental theologian among evangelicals today. But although Thielicke's book *The Ethics of Sex* was published in 1964, it is just now becoming known in evangelical circles for its position regarding homosexuality. As with C. S. Lewis, evangelicals at times overlook divergent opinions of scholars whom they otherwise trust. Such seems to have been the case here, until the recent controversy, that is. In *The Ethics of Sex* Thielicke understands the divine ordering of humanity to be a male-female duality. Thus, homosexuality is not simply a variant of nature but a disturbed relationship resulting from the fall. It is a pathology, a sickness. To begin one's discussion of homosexuality with the orders of creation, however, is easily to overlook the phenomenon itself for the larger patterning. The homosexuals' sickness is easily judged a sin and the homosexuals wrongly condemned for that which transpired apart from their conscious choice. In this way homosexual relations are dismissed in blanket fashion as perverse, though they often authentically reach out for the totality of other human beings. Instead of beginning theoretically with the divine order of human sexuality, Thielicke counsels that theologians must first listen carefully to contemporary opinion to be sure that one's medical, as well as theological, view is not distorted.

Second, Thielicke sees the need to consider afresh the relevant statements of the Bible. Though the male-female duality in Genesis is foundational, Thielicke believes that the specific Biblical injunctions against homosexuality have enough interpretive problems associated with them to give the pastoral counselor "a certain freedom to rethink the subject."[31] Why doesn't the Old Testament, for example, link Sodom any more directly with homosexuality (cf. Isa. 1:10; 3:9; Ezek. 16:49; Jer. 23:14)? Does the role in the ancient cult of the injunctions against homosexuality in the Levitical codes qualify their applicability for today? Could 1 Corinthians 6 and 1 Timothy 1 be referring only to a particular kind of homosexual behavior? Is it significant that Paul uses homosexuality illustratively in Romans 1, rather than substantively? Although Paul and Leviticus clearly reject homosexuality, Thielicke thinks it is somewhat unclear how categorically their condemnation is to be taken.

In treating homosexuality pastorally, Thielicke believes that the counselor must not affirm or idealize what is, in fact, a perversion of God's created order. Instead, the consultant's perversion should be considered an "abnormality" in constitution following from the fall. However, homosexual orientation must be judged ethically neutral, for it occurs apart from conscious choice. The homosexual should be encouraged to seek healing and/or to practice abstinence. But if healing proves impossible and if the gift of celibacy is lacking, then the homosexual should be counseled to seek the "optimal ethical potential of sexual self-realization," i. e., an acceptable homosexual partnership.[32] Such advice is on the borderline of ethical possibilities. However, loving concern for the concrete person demands that such an option exist.

Writing in a much more popular style, Lewis Smedes, in his book *Sex for Christians,* echoes much of Thielicke, though perhaps even more cautiously. Smedes begins by arguing that Christians must affirm that their sexuality belongs to creation itself. Our sexuality is the God-given form we take in life as persons. Yet this sexuality can be distorted. One such distortion Smedes discusses is homosexuality. The case is set up on a theoretical level for Smedes to make a blanket judgment relating to homosexuality; but, like Thielicke, he resists this. Instead, he says:

> Christian moralists, speaking in the twilight of their igno-rance, are often amazingly quick to spell out the exact line of duty for the homosexual person. Karl Barth, for instance, felt quite free to lay down one simple mandate for anyone with this "perversion": let him be converted and turn from his decadent

way of life. This may be theoretically sound admonition—as long as it is abstracted from real persons. It may not be bad ethical judgment; but it is ineffective pastoral counsel.[33]

Seeking to minister to homophobes and homophiles alike, Smedes realizes he risks having his comments "misunderstood by Christian heterosexuals as flabby concession and by homosexuals as unfeeling intolerance."[34] Nevertheless, he proceeds in a pastoral vein, attempting to exercise humility, compassion, and sober moral judgment.

Smedes seeks to steer a course between viewing homosexuality as an alternate form of normal sexuality and as a self-chosen perversion. The informed Christian must reject both assessments, Smedes believes. For regarding the former: (a) the Biblical indicators seem clear in judging homosexual practice as unnatural and godless. Moreover, (b) homosexual activity is only rarely an expression of creative personal relationship. And (c) homosexuality is rarely well integrated into the total development of a person's character. As to the latter, Smedes cautions: "No homosexual, to my knowledge, ever decides to be homosexual; he only makes the painful discovery at one time or another that he is homosexual."[35]

Instead of these two options, which are based in sentiment or revulsion, homosexuals should be counseled to face the abnormality of their condition without feeling guilt for it, but recognizing fully their responsibility for how they make use of their homosexual drives. They should seek change through divine healing or modification of their behavior through counseling. If neither proves possible, the homosexual person should seek an "optimum homosexual morality." To counsel such a course is not "to accept homosexual practices as morally commendable. It is, however, to recognize that the optimum moral life within a deplorable situation is preferable to a life of sexual chaos."[36]

4. Full Acceptance

Thielicke and Smedes see the need to be informed by contemporary opinion concerning homosexuality, both as to the possibility of committed loving relationships (occasional, though rare) and as to the possibility of cure (unlikely). Moreover, they detect a certain ambiguity in those Biblical passages directly mentioning homosexuality, even while asserting heterosexuality to be the wider Biblical norm. Although the Bible considers homosexuality "unnatural" (Rom. 1:26), for example, it makes the same judgment concerning long hair in men (1 Cor. 11:14).[37] What can be concluded? Thielicke and Smedes leave such questions open, but they refuse to stray far from traditional theological judgment.

There are other evangelicals, however, who are willing to entertain much more fully a new theological stance. In their book *Is the Homosexual My Neighbor?—Another Christian View* (1978) co-authors Letha Scanzoni and Virginia Ramey Mollenkott continue to evidence some of the above tentativeness as they couch their conclusions in questions. But the thrust of their writing is distinct from that of either Thielicke or Smedes. They believe that while the Bible clearly condemns certain kinds of homosexual practices ("in the context of gang rape, idolatry, and lustful promiscuity"), *it is silent* concerning both "the idea of a lifelong homosexual orientation" as described by modern behavioral sciences and "the possibility of a permanent, committed relationship of love between homosexuals analogous to heterosexual marriage" as witnessed to by homosexuals' personal testimonies.[38] Recognizing these gaps in the Biblical record, evangelicals must seek to base their theological judgments on sources that are available—personal testimony and informed contemporary opinion, as well as the wider Biblical principle of compassion for the underdog and the Biblical analogue of loving, monogamous heterosexual relationships. In this way Scanzoni and Mollenkott seek to be both faithful to the Biblical witness and honest with the data from our wider culture.

Scanzoni and Mollenkott draw heavily from the social sciences. The heart of their argument hinges on the fact of the homosexual's involuntary orientation. Scientific research shows that there are some persons for whom homosexuality is as "natural" as left-handedness. Certainly God cannot condemn people for an orientation over which they had no choice and which cannot be changed, the authors reason. Furthermore, is it fair to demand of such persons a standard that is more exacting than that for heterosexuals (after all, Paul counsels heterosexuals to marry, rather than "burn")? By insisting that Christian homosexuals either become heterosexual or live celibate forever after, both of which the authors believe to be beyond the capacity of many, aren't Christians driving the homosexual away from the church and toward relationships that tend toward the promiscuous?

Such questions cause Scanzoni and Mollenkott to reevaluate traditional teaching. Peter wrestled with God's call for him to violate Jewish dietary laws which had been ingrained from childhood (Acts 10—11). Huck Finn's friendship with Jim caused him to wrestle with the traditional religious opinion which classified human beings as property. So Christians today must be willing to risk a reassessment of their theological stance concerning homosexuality for the sake of Christian witness and human liberation.

Because we live in a homophobic society, Scanzoni and Mollenkott believe that our Biblical interpretation has been colored accordingly. Although the account in Genesis 19 has made "sodomy" a synonym for homosexuality, the actual offense for which the citizens were punished was one of its perversions—violent homosexual rape. Although Leviticus 18 and 20 prohibit homosexual activity, why is it that prohibitions within the same legal codes that carry the same penalties (cf. not having intercourse during a woman's menstrual period, Lev. 18:19) are ignored by evangelicals today while homosexuality is labeled a vile sin? As for Romans 1, Paul's description does not fit well the case of sincere homosexual Christians who neither worship idols, nor lust in their relationships, nor choose a sexual activity that is contrary to their sexual orientation. 1 Corinthians 6 and 1 Timothy 1 refer perhaps to particular perversions of homosexual practice. The upshot of such reinterpretation of the Biblical texts is to conclude that the Bible is silent regarding exclusive homosexuals and their monogamous relationships.

Not having realized this, Christians have, on the basis of supposed Biblical truth, been "bearing false witness" against their homosexual neighbors. They have claimed that homosexuality is freely chosen and have cruelly held out the hope of cure when such is extremely difficult if not impossible. The church might better open its doors to homosexuals, calling them to monogamous loving relationships. Scanzoni and Mollenkott realize that such a conclusion will surely bring down the scorn of many establishment Christians, but they find encouragement in the fact that some theologians like Smedes and Thielicke are cautiously moving in an accepting direction already. The price of caring will be high, but Jesus' parable of the good Samaritan might serve as a model of courage and of love.

Psychotherapist Ralph Blair is less careful in both his Biblical and theological analyses and more doctrinaire than Scanzoni and Mollenkott concerning scientific evidence, but his conclusions are similar. As president of Evangelicals Concerned (a national task force which has Virginia Mollenkott as its Advisory Board President), Blair has sought to correct traditional judgments in the church toward homosexuality and to organize gay Christians and their supporters. In booklets such as *An Evangelical Look at Homosexuality* (1977, revised) and *Holier-Than-Thou Hocus-Pocus & Homosexuality* (1977), Blair asserts that the Bible does not offer judgment on loving, monogamous homosexual activity between exclusive homosexuals (those with no heterosexual propensity). It is not to the Bible that Christians must turn, for it is silent. Rather Christians need to listen to the social sciences in order to understand better the cause and treatment of homosexuality. Evangelicals must realize that homosexuals do not choose their *orientation;* nor is it susceptible to change.

Blair, like Scanzoni and Mollenkott, enlists Smedes and Thielicke as allies in the battle. But although there are important similarities in their approaches, there is also a fundamental difference: the amount of attention given to the Genesis accounts' description of human sexuality. Blair omits the topic altogether, while Scanzoni and Mollenkott add only a brief postscript to their discussion, admitting that "for many Christians, the biggest barrier to accepting the possibility of homosexual unions pertains to an understanding of the creation accounts in chapters 1, 2, and 5 of Genesis and in Jesus' commentary on them in Matthew, chapter 19."[39] The authors suggest that perhaps "cohumanity," rather than heterosexuality, is the intended focus of these passages, but even they do not find this hypothesis to be totally adequate.

Ralph Blair's writings have been largely ignored by the wider evangelical establishment, but the reviews of Scanzoni and Mollenkott's book reflect the deep-seated controversy which is developing in evangelical circles. Don Williams, writing in *Eternity,* concluded that the book was "polemical apologetics carrying out biased exegesis, selective data and fallacious conclusions."[40] Tim Stafford, on the other hand, writing in establishment evangelicalism's leading journal, *Christianity Today,* had this to say. Scanzoni and Mollenkott

> write in a good Protestant tradition, reevaluating traditional interpretation while holding to the authority of the Scriptures. . . . Most of the people who hate this book will be, I suspect, people who have not read it. One can disagree strongly with its conclusions—I do—and yet wish for more books like its well-documented, compassionate, and courageous style.[41]

Kay Lindskoog on the other hand responded in *The Wittenburg Door:*

> When I finished reading the book I asked myself if practicing homosexuals should be fully accepted into all church positions the same as practicing heterosexuals, with the same standards of fidelity and responsibility applying to both. I felt just like Mark Twain: "I was gratified to be able to answer promptly, and I did. I said I didn't know."[42]

Issues to Be Settled

The above survey indicates that evangelicals have a number of important issues to settle before they can present a theological consensus concerning homosexuality. Evangelicals must settle, first of all, whether observation can, indeed, be a starting point theologically or whether an analysis of Scripture must always initiate the discussion. If observation has a valid role to play in theological formation, what can be said about the possibility of a cure for homosexuality? Again, can theologians make use of the social scientists' distinction between homosexual orientation and homosexual activity, or is such a dichotomy a sub-Biblical rending of actions and attitudes (cf. Jesus' statements regarding lust and adultery)? Concerning Scripture, evangelicals must decide whether texts referring to human sexuality generally or to homosexuality specifically are the proper starting point. Furthermore, they must judge the exegetical validity of the new interpretations surfacing regarding specific passages. It is to these five concerns that we must now turn, as we seek to indicate a possible direction evangelicals might move in their attempt at consensus-building on this issue.

1. One's Starting Point: Revelation or Observation?

Most contemporary evangelical studies of homosexuality begin contextually, relating a personal story or recapping the rise of the gay movement in this country. Yet there is a marked divergence of opinion regarding the usefulness and rightful place of personal, cultural, and scientific observation in the theological process. Lovelace believes " 'the experience of Christian people' is notoriously unreliable as an ethical guide" and " 'the data of the empirical sciences are not directly useful as a source of ethical norms. When it plays by its own rules, science is value free; when it does not, it is misleading," he cautions.[43] Williams is more willing to make use of "man's observation of the human condition," but he too believes it is crucial for Christian theology to *begin* its analysis with God's revelation of his divine will. "Nature, although created by God, does not reveal the unclouded will of God. There is always potential distortion. . . . God's will is not the result of a majority vote," he argues.[44]

Both Williams and Lovelace seem to be confusing one's theological starting point with one's theological norm. Although Barth argued otherwise, most theologians have granted the possibility of nature (through general revelation) serving as a "point of contact" with the divine. As the Christian seeks God's will in his Word regarding the issue of homosexuality, observation (whether personal testimony or scientific analysis) can serve as a guide. Such observation can sharpen our critical evaluations, helping us to overcome our homophobic biases and avoid simplistic and superficial answers. It can set the stage for a responsible Christian response. As David Hubbard counsels:

> Our Christian belief in God as Creator tells us that information gained from human experience or scientific research has a validity to which we should pay attention. Christian revelation is twofold. God speaks through his world and through his Word. The Bible, of course, is the final authority when it comes to Christian belief and Christian conduct, but a solid knowledge of the causes and effects of human behavior can be of substantial help in understanding and applying the teachings of Scripture to our daily living.[45]

Independent of the homosexual controversy, Lovelace and Williams would no doubt agree with Hubbard's statement. But their encounter with gay advocates who claim that what is "natural" must be right and what reflects "love" must be true has caused them to deny cultural observation its initiatory role in this issue. The misuse of empirical data by some has caused Lovelace and Williams wrongly to reject the social sciences as one possible theological point of entry. Theologians need, at times, the instruction and sensitization that careful observation can bring, even while it is recognized that one's decision concerning the will of God will need confirmation, correction, and/or enlightenment through the Scriptures.

There is an ongoing danger in the theological use of observation to be sure. Letha Scanzoni, for example, in a reply to Smedes's discussion of homosexuality in *The Reformed Journal,* makes the mistake of absolutizing experience, arguing that because homosexuals exist and God is sovereign, then they must have "God's express permission."[46] But surely to recognize the existence of a phenomenon (cf. evil) is not to necessitate God's moral approbation of it, as Scanzoni desires. To regard as divinely ordained what a fallen society or a pathological family has produced is to elevate the observation of creation to normative status (cf. Rom. 8:19–22). Under the power of sin, the world's orders, including its sexuality, remain ambiguous.

In his appendix to *The Bond That Breaks,* Williams criticizes the majority report of the Task Force on Homosexuality of the United Presbyterian Church in the U.S.A. He likens those who let scientific study serve as their starting point chronologically with Helmut Thielicke's analysis in *The Evangelical Faith* of "Cartesian theology." Such an approach, he believes, starts with humanity, not with God. But this is to misread Thielicke, again confusing the theological initiator with one's ultimate norm. If one gives paramount importance to empirical "findings"—if one is unwilling, that is, to let the Holy Spirit, working through the Biblical text, toss aside our preliminary observations and questions—then one has fallen prey of what Thielicke labels Cartesianism. But this is by no means necessary; cultural observation need not dictate one's conclusions. Moreover, Thielicke rightfully recognizes that we all have "pre-understandings" based in our social and historical context which we bring to a given subject. These serve for everyone as points of entry as they come to the reading of Scripture. The present situation and its questions, therefore, can be profitably heard, in order that one's pre-understanding be made the more adequate. But, reasons Thielicke, while current questions and self-understanding must be heard, "they must not become a normative principle nor must they be allowed to prejudice the answer; they must be constantly recast and transcended in encounter with the text."[47]

Here is the evangelical's agenda regarding a theology of homosexuality. Listen carefully to the social sciences and to personal testimony, but never permit personal sentiment or intellectual pride to inhibit the recasting and transcendence of human observation through objective encounter with the Spirit in Scripture. Subjective pride and sentiment are a constant danger for both advocates and detractors of a Christian homosexuality. Compassion and revulsion can equally becloud the issue (though the former is certainly more defensible). Arrogance is the temptation of all thoughtful Christians who at times confuse human judgment with divine will. But initial interaction with one's larger culture need not cause such theological pitfalls. It can serve as a positive, informing guide into an otherwise easily confused topic. Such is surely the case in regard to homosexuality.

2. Is a Cure Possible?

The current controversy over the possibility of change in the homosexual's orientation makes starting with human observation all the more problematic for theological discussion. Who is one to believe? Ralph Blair adamantly claims that no exclusive homosexual has ever been cured. "There is not one shred of evidence of a *validated* conversion to *heterosexual orientation* through therapy *or* Christian conversion and prayer," he writes.[48] At the other end of the spectrum, Richard Lovelace claims that homosexuals can, and indeed are being healed and transformed in their sexual orientation, as Paul himself asserts (1 Cor. 6:11), through the full resources of grace available to the Christian.[49]

Who is correct? The answer seems to be neither, completely. Paul did not seemingly have a change in homosexual *orientation* in mind when he wrote to the Corinthians concerning a conversion in their life-style (i. e., *activity*) through Christ and his Spirit. For the presence, medically, of a homosexual orientation seems to have been unknown until a few years prior to the turn of this century, and thus

Scripture remains necessarily silent concerning any direct, non-miraculous cure for it. But Blair is also mistaken, for scientific evidence is not as uniform as he asserts, though documentation of successful therapy is indeed rare. E. Mansell Pattison, a professor of psychiatry at the University of California, Irvine, asserts, in the September 1977 issue of the *Journal of the American Scientific Affiliation,* that a five-year study he has conducted indicates that

> Christian men and women have achieved successful changes in their homosexual orientations, their life-styles, and achieved major emotional and spiritual growth. As a result, much like Alcoholics Anonymous, small cells or groups of "ex-gays" are now offering counseling within the context of a nurturant Christian community, with apparent success.[50]

If this is true, it not only qualifies, but seriously undercuts both Blair's and Scanzoni and Mollenkott's theses. For these writers base much of their argument on the permanency, and thus "naturalness," of one's sexual orientation.

It must also be said, however, that scientific evidence or Biblical revelation does not allow one to hold out the guarantee of a cure at this time for all who desire reorientation of their homosexual propensity. The personal testimony of countless sincere Christian homosexuals, many who were involved in supportive Christian communities, suggests that some exclusive homosexuals might indeed be fixed in their orientation, just as alcoholics remain addicted even when sober. We will need in our discussion of human sexuality below to comment further on this point, for those like Scanzoni and Mollenkott would claim that those without hope of cure shouldn't be denied all sexual outlet. What is at stake in such an evaluation is the nature of "singleness" vis-à-vis God's intended ordering of humanity as male and female. Must one be sexually active to be complete?

3. Can One's Orientation and One's Action Be Separated?

Along with controversy over the possibility of a successful "cure" for the homosexual's orientation, we have noted that questions concerning the cause of homosexuality remain the most perplexing area of homosexual study among scientists. But while its origins remain mysterious, there is near unanimity about the fact that individuals exercise no real personal choice in the development of their sexual *orientation*—heterosexual or homosexual. Both precede the development of any sexual desires or activity. It is knowledge of this fact that has caused contemporary evangelicals like Thielicke to distinguish between a homosexual orientation (usually judged non-condemnatorially) and homosexual practice (usually judged as sinful). Writing in *Moody Monthly,* for example, Kay Oliver and Wayne Christianson conclude: "Though the Bible condemns homosexual practice, it does not condemn the homosexual desire. There's a big difference. The act, not the bent, is the sin."[51] Writing in *Christianity Today,* Episcopal Bishop Bennett Sims makes much the same conclusion, finding in Galatians 5:16 ("walk by the Spirit, and do not gratify the desires of the flesh") evidence that an orientation that is not enacted need not be judged sinful.[52]

Such conclusions have problems, however, as Scanzoni points out. They seem to require a sub-Biblical split between what someone is and how someone lives, between what people *feel* and what people do. Scanzoni writes,

> This [bifurcation] . . . is actually a concession to the weight of scientific evidence that shows that homosexuality is not a willful choice. Accepting the orientation but censuring the act seems compassionate and yet retains an allegiance to traditional interpretations of Scripture regarding the wrongness of homosexual behavior. But I think that approach catches us in a trap. The Scriptures are quite plain in teaching that if an action is wrong, the longing to engage in that action is just as wrong (e.g., Matt. 5:27–28; 1 John 3:15).[53]

To concentrate on actions alone would be legalistic. Scanzoni is correct. But it is perhaps equally mistaken to conflate, as Scanzoni also does, one's orientation with one's feelings and longings. The latter are the result of one's conscious choice to act out internally one's orientation. The former is a product of evil in a fallen world. It is antecedent to choice and, thus, to sinful activity, being one particular manifestation of the fall.

Even as orientation, however, homosexuality is not morally neutral. Dietrich Bonhoeffer's *Ethics* provides a useful discussion in this regard. It distinguishes human guilt (our offense against the divine order) from human sin (our disobedience to the claim of God and of neighbor). Bonhoeffer discusses Jesus in this regard:

> For the sake of God and of men Jesus became a breaker of the law. He broke the law of the Sabbath in order to keep it holy in love for God and for men. He forsook His parents in order to dwell in the house of His Father and thereby to purify His obedience towards His parents. . . . As the one who loved without sin, He became guilty; He wished to share in the fellowship of human guilt; He rejected the devil's accusation which was intended to divert Him from this course.[54]

Jesus took upon himself the guilt of humanity and was, therefore, forsaken by God in his last hour. Yet through this event, he has freed our consciences from the paralysis of guilt so that we might be open for service to God and to our neighbor.

Analogously, the Christian might judge the homosexual's orientation as reflecting the disorder of a fallen world and, as such, producing *guilt.* But only the acting out of this orientation in feelings or deeds would be sinful, that which is contrary to God's simple will for each person's life. One's homosexual orientation produces guilt, for it offends God's intended order of human sexuality. But only one's homosexual activity (whether in thought or deed) can be judged sinful. Moreover, both humanity's guilt (based in our corporate participation and responsibility in a fallen world) and humanity's sin (based in our willful claim to be "like God" and thus able to choose what is right and wrong) are removed by the righteousness of God in Christ Jesus. Though we are all condemned as guilty sinners, we are also free in Christ to live out his desire for our lives.

Instead of judging the homosexual's orientation as "ethically neutral" (something that will be increasingly difficult to communicate pastorally as God's intended order of human sexuality as male and female is understood), the Christian would do better to counsel homosexuals to admit their guilt. Homosexuality is a disordered sexuality, but the righteous judgment of God includes within it his love. God's "no" to sin and guilt remains, but it has been both fully revealed and encompassed by his "yes" on the cross. Guilty, yet forgiven—here is the repentant Christian homosexual's standing with regard to his or her orientation.

4. Human Sexuality or Homosexuality: One's Biblical Starting Point?

The previous questions have challenged differing aspects within each of the three viable theological options for evangelicals concerning homosexuality. Moreover, all have arisen from evidence coming from the social sciences and from the testimony of practicing homosexuals. In a more indirect way, perhaps, such evidence from our larger culture can be seen as important, as well, for an assessment of the proper starting point for Biblical interpretation. For the social sciences are confirming the opinion of some Biblical interpreters that an adequate understanding of homosexuality can only be gained within the larger context of an investigation of human sexuality.

It is a critical weakness in the interpretation of Scanzoni and Mollenkott and Blair that the theological context of homosexuality in human sexuality is almost entirely ignored in their discussions of the Biblical witness. (This is a particularly curious omission in light of the women's excellent discussion of human sexuality in their treatments of women in the church and family. Cf. chapter III.) As Don Williams states:

> If we start our discussion of the Bible with the specific passages on homosexuality (as all gay advocates do) rather than with the opening chapters of Genesis, it is like trying to understand a tree by starting with the branches. Forgetting that the branches come from the trunk, we can dispose of them one by one without ever understanding their origin or their interrelationship. Only as the specific passages on homosexuality, like branches, are related to the trunk of Genesis, do they make a tree.[55]

Without a firm grounding in a Biblical understanding of sexuality (Gen. 1—3; Jesus' commentary on it in Matt. 19; the Song of Solomon), the Biblical texts pertaining to homosexuality are reduced to occasional references which are easily misunderstood.

A lack of attention to the topic of Biblical sexuality also has a second consequence. It ignores the important Biblical perspective that sexual activity is nowhere considered foundational for one's full humanity. If sexual completeness is based in sexual acts, it is unfair to deny homosexuals this expression of their sexuality. If, on the other hand, sexual completeness consists in a healthy interaction of male *or* female as male *and* female, then intercourse is a God-given, but by no means necessary expression. If fulfillment of one's sexual urges is made a prerequisite for the expression of one's full humanity, one is forced to wonder whether Jesus was indeed fully human. Reflection on the Genesis accounts suggests, however, that sexual happiness need not have the added blessing of intercourse. Humanity was created first as male and female in relationship (Gen. 1:27; 2:18–23). Only then were the blessings of procreation (Gen. 1:28) and marriage (Gen. 2:24) added. Our sexual happiness is, thus, not based in either our heterosexual or homosexual unions, but in the normal give and take of male and female together. Here is a perspective that allows a high view of singleness for homosexuals and heterosexuals alike. Without such a starting point, as one grants homosexuals expression of their God-given urges, pressure mounts to be consistent and give the privilege of genital relationships to single heterosexuals with similarly frustrated desires as well. And what of the frustrated married partner who truly falls in love with someone else (e. g. Anna Karenina)?

In response to such criticism, Scanzoni and Mollenkott argue that homosexuals must be distinguished from heterosexual singles for the latter have at least the possibility of sexual fulfillment within marriage. But surely this is merely a "theoretical" possibility for some, given circumstances and personhood. Does the lonely, heterosexual, single male or female with strong sexual urges that are ungratified differ in *practice* from that of the continent single homosexual? Surely it would be wrong to argue that homosexuals *per se* have a higher degree of sexual energy than heterosexuals. A more substantive rebuttal is Scanzoni and Mollenkott's assertion following Thielicke that only with the gift of celibacy freely chosen can abstinence be a creative alternative for fulfilling one's God-intended humanity (here is the exception clause under which Jesus' and Paul's humanity can be viewed). But this again implies that sexual relations are morally justified before marriage and among those who remain single, if the freely chosen gift of celibacy is lacking. However, Scanzoni, in her previous writings on singleness, has not drawn such a conclusion, though consistency would cause one to expect it. She writes,

> Of course, there is no denying that some single persons are persuaded they don't have the gift of singleness, just as some married persons may not have the gift of marriage—and some parents don't have the gift of parenting. Persons may find themselves in any of these categories by force of circumstance rather than by choice or a sense of God's call, and they may need our special love, encouragement, and understanding.[56]

Scanzoni rightly suggests that the situation of singleness demands responsible action, irrespective of special calling or free choice in the matter. It seems true to the Biblical witness to conclude that where responsibility is required (in this case, homosexual continence), there God will supply the "gift." Where discipline proves almost uncontrollably difficult, the special love, encouragement, and counseling of the Christian community will be even more vital.

5. What Do the Biblical Texts Mean?

In his excellent review-article of the books of Scanzoni and Mollenkott and Williams, Tim Stafford comments: "[Scanzoni and Mollenkott] write in a good Protestant tradition, reevaluating traditional interpretation while holding to the authority of the Scriptures. They don't suggest that some biblical commands should be ignored because an ethic of love is more important. Instead they assume that a correct understanding of the biblical commands will identify the meaning of love."[57] While this is indeed true, one is obligated to judge the validity of their interpretations (and those like them) and ask, is the Biblical record interested in prohibiting only certain forms of homosexual abuse while permitting monogamous, loving homosexual unions? In light of current arguments that have surfaced, and upon which Smedes, Thielicke, Scanzoni and Mollenkott, and Blair all draw, the answer seems to be "no." A Biblical case for loving relationships between exclusive homosexuals has not yet been adequately drawn, and even the assertion of Biblical silence and thus indifference on the matter would seem unjustified.

Scanzoni and Mollenkott assert that since the Biblical context of those passages referring to homosexuality is always a negative one (violence, idolatrous worship, promiscuity, adultery), the Bible cannot be judged as providing any information concerning positive homosexual relationships. Certainly some of their argument is convincing. Exegetes have often claimed too much for a text. The Genesis 19 account of Sodom, as Scanzoni and Mollenkott rightly assert, is not about homosexuality in general, but violent homosexual rape for the purpose of humiliating the victim (much like what goes on in our prisons today). Not all of their arguments are convincing (can Jude 7's "unnatural lusts" refer only to the fact that the strangers were "angels"?), but it is nevertheless true that "sodomy" has wrongly been made a synonym for homosexuality.

Concerning Leviticus 18:22 and 20:13, Scanzoni and Mollenkott find the historical context of these prohibitions in the need for ceremonial cleanness and the desire to separate from the fertility cults of Israel's neighbors which used male cult prostitutes. Here their argument is extremely tenuous, for there is no positive evidence for cultic homosexuality in Canaanite religions and such a practice would seem to be nonsensical within those cults which sought to use the sympathetic magic of male-female intercourse to arouse the fertility of the gods. Although the texts that are used as support (Deut. 23:17–19; 1 Kings 14:24; 2 Kings 23:7) indeed seem to refer to male "cult prostitutes" (cf. the RSV translation), this is a mistranslation of the Hebrew word *qadesh*. The root meaning of the word *qadesh* is "sacred," referring in this context to those who worked in the non-Jewish temples. And while the female *qadesh(ah)* had sexual duties, the male *qadesh* were rather priests with other functions in the cult.

A stronger argument for relativizing the blanket injunction against homosexuality in Leviticus is the inconsistency with which the Levitical code is followed today in evangelical circles. Why is it that evangelicals ignore the prohibition against intercourse with a woman during her menstrual period (Lev. 20:18) or the prohibition against rare steaks? Although the issue is complex, the answer can perhaps be given that it is because the New Testament nowhere relativizes or qualifies the injunctions against homosexuality as it does the others that are mentioned (cf. Mark 5:25–34; Col. 2:16). Again, it is the case that the Old Testament presents heterosexuality as the norm (Gen. 1 —3; Song of Solomon). Finally, the New Testament explicitly labels homosexual activity as sinful.

The context of Romans 1 is not simply individual lust and idolatry among those denying their "nature" (i. e., their heterosexual orientation). It is rather the fall and its resultant disorder—toward God (1:19–23), within ourselves (1:24–27), and toward others (1:28–31). Paul is arguing that we are all sinners and he uses homosexuality as an illustration of how this perverts our intended humanity. Homosexuality is certainly not the worst sin or even a "signal" sin. It is only one example of our chaos that the fall provoked. Such a judgment is also borne out in Paul's catalogue of vices in 1 Corinthians 6:9, 10 and 1 Timothy 1:8–11. Scanzoni and Mollenkott point out that in the Corinthians text, the two Greek words which are combined and rendered simply "sexual perverts" in the RSV translation *(malakoi* and *arsenokoitai)* are obscure in their meaning and might refer only to specific kinds of homosexual abuse. But even Scanzoni and Mollenkott leave such a judgment as a largely unsupported possibility. To sum up, there is contrary evidence from the texts which counters Scanzoni and Mollenkott's position.

Finally, there remains the fundamental fact that there is no positive Scriptural support for even a qualified homosexuality. In the somewhat analogous situations of slavery and feminism, where long-cherished positions of Biblical interpretation were shown to be erroneous, there were supporting Biblical data to assist one's evaluation (e. g. Gal. 3:28; Gen. 1:27). But no one is seriously claiming among evangelicals that Scripture in any way explicitly supports a homosexual union. Ruth and Naomi, and David and Jonathan are mentioned as Biblical models in non-evangelical circles, but the lack of textual support for such claims has kept evangelicals from enlisting these in their cause.

Bound up with a Biblical doctrine of the human, rooted in the order of creation, spelled out by the Law, and reinforced by Paul's treatment of both the Law (1 Tim. 1) and the kingdom of God (1 Cor. 6), the Biblical mandate against homosexuality seems strong. While

new evidence might be forthcoming which would alter this assessment, it is not, at present, available.

Conclusions

Perhaps after reading this chapter some are asking, "If the result
of this discussion is merely the reaffirmation of traditional theological
judgments, what has been gained?" Has interaction with our contemporary culture proven instructive in any way to the theological task?
While it would seem that the overall evaluation of homosexuality as
a deviation from God's intended order of human sexuality should
remain unchanged, the current ferment is nevertheless contributing to
the theological task of the church in several important ways.

First, the current controversy is pointing out the existence of a
widespread homophobia (fear and/or disgust of homosexuality)
among evangelicals. This must be eliminated if the Bible is to remain
the sole norm of faith and life in the church. As we have seen, there
is no Biblical support for singling out homosexuality as uniquely
offensive to God or harmful to people. It is one sin among many. To
argue, as Lovelace does, that the sin of homosexuality is the lid to
Pandora's box, which, once opened, leads both to widespread perversion and "paganism," is both sub-Biblical and without adequate historical support. To be rejected, as well, is the sensationalist discussion
in otherwise serious literature that would, for example, compare the
sexual appetite of homosexuals to "starving people in besieged cities
of the past" who "found their mouths watering for such delicacies as
boiled rats."[58] An evangelical theology must be based in a genuine
Christian response to homosexual persons, not in a revulsion or fear-
ful recoil. As a sign of the church's penitence in this matter, it might
begin by removing from its informal vocabulary words such as
"queers," "fags," "fairies," "homos," "perverts," and the like.
Though the term is unsuitable in many ways, "gay" remains a better
informal designation for the homosexual and lesbian, for, because it
is the homosexuals' self-designation, it suggests the church's acceptance of their personhood.

Second, current theological debate is demonstrating the need for
the correction of widespread ignorance among evangelicals on the

topic of homosexuality. This misinformation pertains both to the cultural data and to the Biblical record. Although evangelicals might have been correct in their basic assessment of homosexuality's sin, they have been guilty of false argument and misstatement in much of their theological discussion. Sodom cannot be used to justify homosexuality's "detestable" character. Nor can the notion of "choice" be simplistically asserted as justifying homosexuals' responsibility concerning the adoption of their sexual orientation. Evangelicals need to bury these and similar "myths," repenting of the smugness in which they have often dealt with the topic in the past.

Finally, the theological controversy concerning homosexuality can provide evangelicals a model for the handling of theological issues in other areas of faith and life as well. How should one respond to continuing input from the broader culture? Certainly openness and humility are demanded. Prejudices and misconceptions need correction. Hurtful responses demand repentance and, wherever possible, restitution. Beyond this, the controversy concerning homosexuality leaves one with the awareness that the burden of proof remains on those proposing theological change. Authors like Scanzoni and Mollenkott are to be commended for the courageous and compassionate manner in which they have explored the issue of homosexuality. Although evidence is lacking for any major redirection in theological judgment, their work might yet prove helpful to evangelicals in moving beyond petrified opinion. Until evidence surfaces, evangelicals should gratefully receive the corrections gay advocates can offer, while continuing to assert in love that the traditional position concerning the sinfulness of all homosexual activity is true to the Biblical norm.

VI

Constructive
Evangelical Theology

The topics dealt with in the preceding chapters—inspiration, women, social ethics, and homosexuality—are important beyond their immediate purview. Collectively they raise the issue of theological interpretation among evangelicals. Moreover, they do so in a way that is current and accessible, focusing upon concerns of the entire church. They help to define the nature of evangelicalism's theological impasse in a way that the average Christian churchgoer who reflects on the faith can understand. It should be apparent to all who have read this far that evangelicals are suffering from a crisis in their basic theological method. Although Biblical authority is asserted as a hallmark of the movement, it is daily called into question by the independent and contradictory theological opinions which are being given dogmatic status by evangelical writers.

A Criticism of Evangelical Theology

In his critique of American evangelicalism, James Barr comments on the fact that "conservatives have been on the whole a remarkably quarrelsome segment of Christendom." He observes that marked conflicts and tensions lie at the heart of the movement, though an outsider might imagine that the "conservative evangelical faith possesses a monolithic unity."[1] We have seen in the chapters above that Barr is correct in his assessment. Barr, an Englishman, far removed from American evangelicalism both geographically and theologically, illustrates his contention by discussing the perennial issues of Calvinism/Arminianism, Millennialism, and Pentecostalism. I have centered my thinking in this book on some of the more immediate theological controversies that are causing ferment in the evangelical world. Other issues no doubt could have been chosen. David Hubbard, for example, in his taped remarks on the future of evangelicalism to a colloquium at Conservative Baptist Theological Seminary in Denver in 1977 noted the following areas of tension among evangelicals: women's ordination, the charismatic movement, ecumenical relations, social ethics, strategies of evangelism, Biblical criticism, Biblical infallibility, contextual theology in non-Western cultures, and the churchly applications of the behavioral sciences.[2] If such a list is more exhaustive than those topics which this book has pursued, it nevertheless makes it clear that the foci of the preceding chapters have at least been representative.

Contemporary evangelicals are finding it difficult to achieve anything like consensus on each succeeding theological topic they address. Moreover, they seem to be stymied in any effort toward unity, unable to agree on a collective interpretive strategy for moving beyond their current impasse. But surely a commitment to Biblical authority is a commitment to take this *common* task of theological interpretation seriously—more seriously than many are at present doing. It is a commitment to hold together with those who share a similar norm, to carry on mature conversations, to affirm a oneness in the gospel, while working on the issues that currently divide.[3] Evangelicals need the collective wisdom of their best minds and spirits working together on the theological task of the church. Problems in theological formulation will prove ongoing, but the interpretive project "will have a much better chance of success in the clear air of fellowship than in an atmosphere fouled by competition."[4]

The common interpretive task entails risk, but such is a necessary ingredient of a commitment to Biblical authority. As G.C. Berkouwer has recognized,

> To confess Holy Scripture and its authority is to be aware of the command to understand and to interpret it. It always places us at the beginning of a road that we can only travel in "fear and trepidation."[5]

Unfortunately, some evangelicals have viewed this common road of theological interpretation as being too risky to travel. For this reason they have retrenched into what Berkouwer calls "a biblicist misinterpretation of the church's dealings with Scripture and its confession."[6] Interpretations have seemed to lead in questionable directions—directions which either have moved away from traditional Biblical consensus or have disputed current cultural analysis. A concern for social ethics, for example, has seemed to some a forfeiture of the desire to preach to the lost. An interest in ministering to the hurts of homosexuals has been interpreted as becoming theologically "soft." A willingness to ordain women has been judged a flouting of Biblical truth. At the other end of the evangelical spectrum, we have noted some who are considering portions of the Bible to be erroneous, given the conflict of traditional interpretations on the one hand, and contemporary judgments concerning women on the other. This, too, is a "biblicist misinterpretation." So is the premature judgment that there is "error" in the intended message of the Biblical writers at such other points as the Israelite conquest of Canaan (Josh. 10:40) and David's taking of a census (2 Sam. 24:1-2). Evangelicals must commit themselves to the ongoing, corporate theological task. They must not opt out of the interpretive struggle, believing the project either unnecessary or hopeless.

A commitment to interpretation will always allow the "inadequate" opinions of others a freedom of expression. This is not to adopt a "low" view of Scripture or an "uninformed" approach to theology. It is to take one's commitment to Biblical authority with increased seriousness. The Faculty and Trustee Committee at Fuller Seminary, for example, which investigated Paul Jewett's book *Man as Male and Female* recognized Jewett's commitment to the full authority of Scripture, as well as his important contribution to a theology of women, even while it challenged his handling of the evidence. Censorship will never prove an adequate method for achieving theological consensus. Karl Barth, who changed the direction of twentieth-century theology with his recognition of the bankruptcy of nineteenth-century liberalism, nevertheless did not ignore the theological discussion of those whose understanding of the faith he judged to be inadequate. In his introduction to a study of theology in the last two hundred years, he commented:

"The theology of every age must be sufficiently strong and free to hear, calmly, attentively, and openly, not only the voices of the Church Fathers, not only the voices of its favorites, not only the voices of classical antiquity, but all the voices of the past in its entirety. We cannot prescribe who among the collaborators of the past will be welcomed to participate in our own work, and who will not be. For there is always the possibility that in one sense or another we may be in particular need of wholly unexpected voices, and that among them there may be voices which are at first entirely unwelcome."[7]

What Barth recognized, evangelicals must now affirm, particularly regarding those who share a similar commitment to the Bible as sole authority. And how much easier such dialogue *should be* where there is a common understanding of so much of the gospel message.

New interpretive possibilities for traditional theological judgments must be encouraged. To contend for change as some evangelicals are doing on each of the topics we have explored is not necessarily to play "fast and loose" with Biblical authority. It might be the case on a particular issue, as the topic of women in the church is currently indicating, that traditionalists are the ones who have misinterpreted the Biblical posture. It might also be true, as with the discussion of homosexuality, that revisionists are straying from the Biblical norm. But both traditionalists and revisionists can share in common a commitment to the full authority of Scripture in faith and life, and the vast majority of those who call themselves evangelicals do just that. It is not the occurrence, or lack thereof, of traditional theological opinion that will guarantee Biblical authority, but the common commitment of the evangelical community to work together at the interpretive task.

The "Art" of Evangelical Theology

General consensus is the goal of that risky, communal process of theological interpretation. Obviously, unified opinion does not happen by fiat. It is much more difficult to say, however, how such an end is achieved. Theological interpretation is not only a science, but an art. It is a "science" in that its sources and their relations lend themselves to careful analysis, deduction and critique—whether these be Biblical, traditional, or contemporary. Operational suggestions concerning the theological task can be offered as the preceding pages have done. But while methodological questions must be considered carefully, one must remember, at the same time, that, as Bernard Lonergan has observed, theological "method is not a set of rules to be followed meticulously by a dolt. It is a framework for collaborative creativity."[8] Theology remains an "art" in that the proper valuation and interaction of its sources demand a wisdom that defies a comprehensive codification. As John Leith suggests,

> Theology is wisdom, not precisely defined scientific knowledge. Just as there is a human wisdom that comes with maturity and is the result of the interaction of experience and critical reflection, so there is a theological wisdom that comes with maturity and is the result of the interaction of critical reflection, of experience in the church, of engagement with Scripture, of Christian witness today, and of the testimony of the Holy Spirit.[9]

Leith continues, quoting Joseph Sittler with approval:

> My own disinclination to state a theological method is grounded in the strong conviction that one does not devise a method and then dig into the data; one lives with the data, lets their force, variety, and authenticity generate a sense for what Jean Danielou calls a "way of knowing" appropriate to the nature of the data.[10]

Living with the data and letting them suggest the theological agenda ahead has been the method I have taken in the chapters just concluded. In each case the result has been that a differing approach has surfaced. While Biblical hermeneutics provided the key to an understanding of the role of women in the church and family, dialogue between those whose traditions have heard the Word of God differently in other times and places held the key for the discussion of social ethics, and engagement with the full range of cultural activity (from psychotherapy to radical protest, from personal testimony to scientific statement) was the locus for theological evaluation concerning homosexuality. As for the topic of inspiration, the issues that are proving central find their interim "solutions" in all three of theology's resources. The evangelical should view such differences in theological method as signifying a health in the creative process, rather than a

confusion over technique. Moreover, the evangelical should be open
to the revision of even these approaches, realizing with Barth that the
theological task must be carried out " 'in full earnestness again and
again, indeed beginning from the beginning.' "[11]

Theology's Sources as Threefold

To begin one's theological interpretations afresh, as I have attempted in this book, demands a careful, creative, communal listening
to the theological sources. For theology is the translation of Christian
truth into contemporary idiom with an eye toward Biblical foundations, traditional formulations, and contemporary judgments. It is the
existence of these differing sources that makes the matter of interpretation, or hermeneutics, so crucial. The word "hermeneutics" (Greek,
hermeneuein), as used in the New Testament, means to expound or
to translate. It is particularly in the latter sense of translation, or
"bridging the gap" (Berkouwer), that the theologian is indeed a
hermeneutician.[12] Theologians must build bridges with their interpretations between the Biblical writers, the church fathers, and contemporary Christians. Their interpretations will succeed only if they are
based on the sound analysis of their constitutive theological components.[13]

Evangelicals have rightly valued the Bible as God's-Word-in-
human-words. Because it is "God's Word," it is the ultimate norm of
evangelical theology. One's order of theological discovery or order of
theological presentation must never cause confusion as to the source
of one's final authority. But even if *Scripture* is used to initiate the
theological process or presentation, the chance of confusion remains.
For the Bible is also human words, and thus demands a proper
reading and understanding. Surely "knowing how the Bible wants to
be heard is as important as defending its authority" as God-given.[14]
We have seen in chapter III how this is indeed the case.

Perhaps the key issue in allowing Scripture to be heard on its own
terms is the recognition that the Biblical interpreter is a bridge-
builder. Theologians who come to Scripture must overcome the gap
that separates their world from that of the Biblical writers—a gap that
involves language, thought-forms, cultural practices, and historical

situations. Commenting on Calvin's recognition of this fact, Barth wrote:

> how energetically Calvin, having first established what stands in the text, sets himself to re-think the whole material and to wrestle with it, till the walls which separate the sixteenth century from the first become transparent! Paul speaks, and the man of the sixteenth century hears. The conversation between the original record and the reader moves round the subject-matter, until a distinction between yesterday and today becomes impossible.[15]

Evangelicals believe that the Biblical writers know of God what others do not know; and their writings allow others to know what they knew. But only through an openness to Biblical scholarship and a willingness to undertake fresh exegesis can that authoritative message be heard in our day. As John Robertson said centuries ago, " 'God has yet more truth to break forth from His Holy Word.' "[16]

We have seen in chapter IV that *tradition* is a second source for contemporary evangelical theology. To reject the task of Biblical hermeneutics would be theological suicide. But to isolate conclusions concerning Biblical interpretation from the theological judgments and experience of the Christian community through the ages is almost as unsatisfactory. As Leith comments,

> The Christian community has a theological maturity and an historical discernment that should not be easily surrendered and which should impinge upon all technical studies of the Scriptures. Augustine, Luther, Calvin, the English Puritans, and Kierkegaard, among others, read Scripture with a profundity of understanding that has not been surpassed by those who are the beneficiaries of modern critical studies.[17]

Even as evangelical theology is done "again and again" in each succeeding generation, it should not start from scratch. Rather it should attempt to translate the truth of previous ages into contemporary expression. It must examine critically and gratefully all that has come before. If, after careful analysis, it concludes that some part of the corporate convictions of the community of the faithful through the ages must be rejected, it accepts the fact that the burden of proof concerning such change lies on its own shoulders.

In addition to the need to listen both to the Bible and to tradition, we have seen in chapter V that the evangelical theologian must also listen to the *world.* Some evangelicals have been particularly resistive at this point, but, as even Calvin recognized, they need not be. Not only was Calvin's theology Biblical and traditional, but it sought to build bridges between it and the larger secular humanist culture. In his *Institutes,* Calvin argues:

> Whenever we come upon these matters in secular writers, let that admirable light of truth shining in them teach us that the mind of man, though fallen and perverted from its wholeness, is nevertheless clothed and ornamented with God's excellent gifts.[18]

It is true, perhaps, that Calvin was guilty of deciding prior to his interaction with the wider culture what was to be considered Christian truth. The danger of such a procedure is a selective listening to non-Christian sources. Rather than hearing secular culture on its own terms, Christians are tempted to lift from it only those things that are congenial to their particular traditional viewpoint. In the process, cultural insight is short-shrifted and evangelical theology consequently impoverished.[19] But Calvin was correct, at least, in recognizing the need to make use of non-Christian sources.

Evangelicals can learn in our own day, perhaps, from Robert McAfee Brown, who has argued strongly for the importance of cultural input for the theological equation. In his book *The Pseudonyms of God* (i. e., those ways God is speaking to us through the disguise of human culture and natural event), Brown argues that "traffic between the gospel and the world travels on a two-way street." He states:

> The gospel helps to inform and define the world, but *the world helps to inform and define the gospel.* I need more than the resources of Bible, theological tradition, and my own commitments if I am to understand my faith and the world in which it is set; I also need the ethical insights of my secular colleagues, the political and psychological analyses of my friends and foes, and the prophetic jab of nonchurchmen whose degree of commitment so often puts my own to shame.[20]

Brown is not arguing for a natural theology—one that would seek to build from humanity to God, or for destroying the infinitely qualitative distinction between the two. Rather he is recognizing that within human life and culture the theologian can get evidence of the divine reality with which the resources of Scripture and tradition can creatively interact. Evangelicals have, unfortunately, failed all too often to make use of the world as a third God-given source for theological creativity.

There are occasions, as we have seen in chapter V, when an evangelical theology will begin with culture and not God. But one's starting point in the knowing-process need not, and must not, be confused with one's ultimate theological authority. A cultural starting point might well demand a "hermeneutical suspicion" (i. e., a distrust of one's previous reading of Scripture, given the possibility that such a reading conceals some of the radical implications of the Biblical message for our day), but it may also assist in the renewed hermeneutical task, allowing the Biblical witness to be freshly experienced, freshly understood, and freshly applied.[21]

Evangelical theology will prove itself to be adequate only as proper attention is given to each of the three theological resources, though no set of rules can be laid down which would guarantee successful interaction among them. All one can say is that the creative dialogue will seek to build bridges between Scripture and church and world in a way appropriate to the particular subject matter in view. Here again we are faced with the realization that evangelical theology is at its best an "art"; it is an entrusting to words what has been creatively perceived in the dialogue among Scripture, church, and world.

The Theologian's Posture

Although the theologian cannot be programmed for success, any more than an artist can paint by number, there are several guidelines concerning the theologian's setting and posture that can be offered by way of conclusion. Certainly chief among these is the need to recognize theology as the perennial task *of the church and for the church*. As I have argued throughout this book, theology must be done in community, not competition. The present pluralism-in-isolation which characterizes much of evangelical thought must give way, as an initial step in the consensus-building process, to a pluralism-in-dialogue.[22] Diversity must be faced openly and in love, as evangelicals together seek theological consensus. Moreover, even an evangelical consensus should not be viewed as an end in itself, but rather as a tool for the church to use in the strengthening of its faith and life. "The theologian's task," as John Calvin recognized "is not to divert the ears with chatter, but to strengthen consciences by teaching things true, sure, and profitable."[23]

Second, theology must be done *in prayer.* As should be already apparent, I have found in the writings of Karl Barth helpful suggestions concerning theological methodology which can prove useful to the evangelical theologian. Although there are other points on which evangelicals would disagree with Barth, certainly evangelicals can profit from his awareness of prayer's indispensable role in the theological task:

> "The first and basic act of theological work is *prayer.* Prayer must, therefore, be the keynote of all that remains to be discussed. . . . theological work does not merely begin with prayer and is not merely accompanied by it; in its totality it is peculiar and characteristic of theology that it can be performed only in the act of prayer. In view of the danger to which theology is exposed and to the hope that is enclosed within its work, it is natural that without prayer there can be no theological work."[24]

Because the subject matter of theology is the Word of God—his address to us—and because theology must always be understood as response—as thinking God's thoughts after him—it must necessarily be an act of prayer itself.

Moreover, because the prayerful response is made by finite people, because theologians are overwhelmed by the magnitude of what they have received, their theological constructions must be put forward *humbly.* Theology must never claim too much for itself. Again, Karl Barth can offer sage advice to his evangelical colleagues, as in this reaction to the success of his own *Church Dogmatics:*

> "The angels laugh at old Karl. They laugh at him because he tries to grasp the truth about God in a book of Dogmatics. They laugh at the fact that volume follows volume and each is thicker than the previous one. As they laugh, they say to one another, 'Look! Here he comes now with his little pushcart full

of volumes of the Dogmatics!' And they laugh about the men who write so much about Karl Barth instead of writing about the things he is trying to write about. Truly, the angels laugh."[25]

Theologians who think too highly of their own meager efforts at capturing the truth of a transcendent God have never fully been overcome by the subject matter they are addressing. Prayer and humility are reverse sides of a correct theological posture.

To seek prayerfully and humbly within the believing community a consensus theology, one arising out of Biblical, traditional, and contemporary data, is the evangelical's task. Only in this way can the current impasse in regard to Biblical authority be overcome. Only in this way will the evangelical church prove itself to be a continuing authentic witness to the Christian faith in the days ahead.

A Postscript

Perhaps a final, qualifying note is in order concerning this book. No doubt many readers have been thinking, can anyone seriously hold up "consensus" as the theological posture for the evangelical world? Isn't theological diversity central to its life, ever since its modern inception on the American scene thirty years ago? To argue for consensus would seem either foolhardy or arrogant—perhaps both.

It is true that evangelicals must learn to live with their differences. This is what it means to do *church* theology. But traditional differences in theological viewpoint between evangelicals have perhaps deadened the evangelicals' resolve to seek unity in their thought. It has caused a commitment to Biblical authority to be divorced wrongly from a commitment to the *common* interpretive task. A pragmatic alliance of silence has evolved within evangelicalism with the result that its basic commitment to Biblical authority now stands threatened. Although differences of opinion are both unavoidable and to be encouraged, they must be viewed as an interim stage on the way toward a point of consensus, which itself must then be challenged on the way toward some future consensus. Without some such resolve, evangelicals will find their paradigms of Biblical authority ringing increasingly hollow.

Notes

Chapter I: The Nature of the Impasse

1. Harold Lindsell, *The Battle for the Bible* (Grand Rapids: Zondervan, 1976).
2. Carl F. H. Henry, *Evangelicals in Search of Identity* (Waco: Word Books, 1976), p. 96.
3. Richard Quebedeaux, *The Young Evangelicals: Revolution in Orthodoxy* (New York: Harper & Row, 1974). Cf. his *The Worldly Evangelicals* (New York: Harper & Row, 1978) for a slightly different classification.
4. Anna B. Warner, "Jesus Loves Me" in *The Little Golden Book of Hymns,* ed. Elsa Jane Werner (Racine, Wis.: Western Publishing Co., 1976), pp. 6–7.
5. Numerical estimates vary, but cf. "Back to That Oldtime Religion," *Time,* 26 December 1977, p. 53.
6. Carl F. H. Henry in "Interview: Carl Henry on Evangelical Identity," *Sojourners* 5 (April 1976):27. Cf. Richard J. Coleman, *Issues of Theological Warfare* (Grand Rapids: Eerdmans, 1972), p. 27; Peter Toon, "The Nature of Evangelicalism—An Anglican Perspective," *The Reformed Journal* 24 (December 1974):27; Virginia R. Mollenkott, "Evangelicalism: A Feminist Perspective," *Union Seminary Quarterly Review* 32 (Winter 1977):95.
7. John Stott, "The Evangelical View of Authority," *Bulletin of Wheaton College* 45 (February 1968):1.
8. Cf. Loraine Boettner, "Evangelical" in *Baker's Dictionary of Theology,* ed. E. F. Harrison (Grand Rapids: Baker Book House, 1960), p. 200; and Clark Pinnock, "Three Views of the Bible in Contemporary Theology" in *Biblical Authority,* ed. Jack Rogers (Waco: Word Books, 1977), p. 60.
9. John Stott, *Understanding the Bible* (Glendale, Calif.: Regal Books, 1972), p. 202.
10. Kenneth Kantzer, "Christ and Scripture," *His* 26 (January 1966):16–20; James Packer, "Calvin's View of Scripture" in *God's Inerrant Word,* ed. John Montgomery (Minneapolis: Bethany Fellowship, 1974), pp. 95–114; Edward John Carnell, *The Case for Orthodox Theology* (Philadelphia: The Westminster Press, 1959), pp. 33–49.

11. Geoffrey W. Bromiley, "The Inspiration & Authority of Scripture," *Eternity,* August 1970, pp. 12–20.

12. Francis Schaeffer, *No Final Conflict: The Bible Without Error in All That It Affirms* (Downers Grove, Ill.: Inter-Varsity Press, 1975), p. 13: "it is the watershed of the evangelical world." Lindsell, *The Battle for the Bible,* p. 210: "I do not for one moment concede, however, that in a technical sense anyone can claim the evangelical badge once he has abandoned inerrancy."

13. Carl F. H. Henry in "Interview: Carl Henry on Evangelical Identity," p. 27; Bernard Ramm, "Is 'Scripture Alone' the Essence of Christianity?" in *Biblical Authority,* ed. Rogers, p. 112; Clark Pinnock, "Foreword" to Stephen T. Davis, *The Debate About the Bible* (Philadelphia: The Westminster Press, 1977), p. 11.

14. Cf. Bernard Ramm, *The Pattern of Religious Authority* (Grand Rapids: Eerdmans, 1959).

15. Clark Pinnock, "The Inerrancy Debate Among the Evangelicals," *Theology, News and Notes* (1976, Special Issue), p. 13 (Pinnock's emphasis).

16. Bromiley, "The Inspiration & Authority of Scripture," p. 19.

17. Dick France, "It Is Written," *Themelios* 2 (May 1977):65.

18. John Stott, *Christ the Controversialist* (Downers Grove, Ill.: Inter-Varsity Press, 1970), p. 44.

19. Lindsell, *The Battle for the Bible,* pp. 177–179. Cf. Dewey M. Beegle, *Scripture, Tradition, and Infallibility* (Grand Rapids: Eerdmans, 1973), pp. 60–63.

20. Paul Holmer, *C. S. Lewis: The Shape of His Faith and Thought* (New York: Harper & Row, 1976), pp. 94, 97, 100.

21. C. S. Lewis, *Reflections on the Psalms* (New York: Harcourt, Brace & World, 1958), pp. 20ff. See also his *God in the Dock* (Grand Rapids: Eerdmans, 1970), pp. 234ff.

22. James Packer, " 'Sola Scriptura' in History and Today" in *God's Inerrant Word,* ed. John Montgomery, p. 56.

23. Pinnock, "The Inerrancy Debate Among the Evangelicals," p. 13.

24. James D. Smart, *The Interpretation of Scripture* (Philadelphia: The Westminster Press, 1961), p. 183. Cf. Karl Barth, *The Epistle to the Romans,* trans. Edwyn Hoskyns (New York: Oxford University Press, 1968), pp. 7–8.

25. Carl F. H. Henry in "The Battle for the Bible: An Interview with Dr. Carl F. H. Henry," *Scribe,* Spring 1976, p. 4.

26. Lindsell, *The Battle for the Bible,* pp. 21, 136, 157, 204.

27. *Ibid.,* p. 38.

28. Mollenkott, "Evangelicalism: A Feminist Perspective," pp. 95, 97–98.

29. Donald Dayton, "Annotations," *Sojourners* 6 (November 1977):36–37.

Chapter II: The Debate over Inspiration: Scripture as Reliable, Inerrant, or Infallible?

1. "New Dispute Looms over 'Errors' in Scripture," *Christianity Today* 7 (April 26, 1963):29.

2. Cf. James Barr, *Fundamentalism* (London: SCM Press, 1977), p. 1; Sydney Ahlstrom, "From Puritanism to Evangelicalism: A Critical Perspective" in *The Evangelicals,* ed. David F. Wells and John D. Woodbridge (Nashville: Abingdon, 1975), p. 270; Martin E. Marty, "Tensions Within Contemporary Evangelicalism: A Critical Appraisal" in *The Evangelicals,* p. 173.

3. Clark Pinnock, "The Inerrancy Debate Among the Evangelicals," *Theology, News and Notes* (1976, Special Issue), p. 11. His quotation is from Edward John Carnell, *The Case for Orthodox Theology* (Philadelphia: The Westminster Press, 1959), p. 13.

4. G. C. Berkouwer, *Holy Scripture,* trans. Jack Rogers (Grand Rapids: Eerdmans, 1975), p. 143.

5. Cf. F. F. Bruce who deplores the "Maginot-line mentality where the doctrine of Scripture is concerned." F. F. Bruce, "Foreword" to Dewey M. Beegle, *Scripture, Tradition, and Infallibility* (Grand Rapids: Eerdmans, 1973), p. 10. Cf. also Helmut Thielicke who was unable to dialogue creatively on the question "Are there errors in the Bible?" which was asked during his visit to the United States in 1963. Helmut Thielicke, *Between Heaven and Earth* (New York: Harper & Row, 1965), pp. 1–13.

6. Gerald T. Sheppard, "Biblical Hermeneutics: The Academic Language of Evangelical Identity," *Union Seminary Quarterly Review* 32 (Winter 1977):84, 88.

7. Cf. the special edition of *Theology, News and Notes* (1976) which was entitled "The Authority of Scripture at Fuller."

8. David Hubbard, "The Current Tensions: Is There a Way Out?" in *Biblical Authority,* ed. Jack Rogers (Waco: Word Books, 1977), p. 176.

9. Edward Carnell, *The Case for Orthodox Theology,* p. 110.

10. "Council Maps 10–Year Push for 'Historic, Verbal' Inerrancy," *Eternity,* November 1977, pp. 10, 90.

11. "A Campaign for Inerrancy," *Christianity Today* 22 (November 4, 1977):51–52; "Council Maps 10–Year Push for 'Historic, Verbal' Inerrancy," p. 90.

12. "Council Maps 10–Year Push for 'Historic, Verbal' Inerrancy," p. 90.

13. Francis Schaeffer, *No Final Conflict: The Bible Without Error in All That It Affirms* (Downers Grove, Ill.: Inter-Varsity Press, 1975), pp. 8, 46, 45.

14. Harold Lindsell, *The Battle for the Bible* (Grand Rapids: Zondervan, 1976), pp. 34–35, 40–71, 162, 171, 182. Though this book has been widely panned and lamented by book reviewers, it remains

significant because of the author's position at the time of publication as editor of *Christianity Today,* because of Harold Ockenga's foreword (he is president of Gordon-Conwell Seminary and a founder of the National Association of Evangelicals), and because of Billy Graham's informal endorsement as quoted in the press. Reviewers have noted the book's anti-intellectualism in terms of higher Biblical criticism, its faulty historical methodology, its lack of candor in stating its own qualifications on the word "inerrancy," and its unwillingness to treat hermeneutics as an issue. Cf. Bernard Ramm, "Misplaced Battle Lines" (review of *The Battle for the Bible* by Harold Lindsell), *The Reformed Journal* 26 (July-August 1976): 37–38; Donald Dayton, "Wrong Front" (review of *The Battle for the Bible* by Harold Lindsell), *The Other Side,* May-June 1976, pp. 36–39; "The Battle for the Bible: An Interview with Dr. Carl F. H. Henry," *Scribe,* Spring 1976, pp. 3–4; Clark Pinnock, "Acrimonious Debate on Inerrancy" (review of *The Battle for the Bible* by Harold Lindsell), *Eternity,* June 1976, pp. 40–41; David Hubbard, "Reflections on Fuller's Theological Position and Role in the Church," paper presented at Seminary Convocation, Fuller Theological Seminary, Pasadena, California, April 8, 1976 (mimeographed).

15. Lindsell, *The Battle for the Bible,* pp. 24, 25, 39, 120–121, 159–160, 203, 206, 210.

16. *Ibid.,* p. 36.

17. *Ibid.,* pp. 175, 168, 166.

18. James Packer, "Calvin's View of Scripture" in *God's Inerrant Word,* ed. John Montgomery (Minneapolis: Bethany Fellowship, 1974), p. 97.

19. Lindsell, *The Battle for the Bible,* pp. 43, 47ff. Cf. Norman Geisler, "The Nature of Scripture" (review of *Biblical Authority,* ed. Jack Rogers), *Christianity Today* 22 (February 24, 1978):34–36.

20. Clark Pinnock, "In Response to Dr. Daniel Fuller," *Journal of the Evangelical Theological Society* 16 (Spring 1973):72.

21. Cf. Roger Nicole, "The Inspiration of Scripture: B. B. Warfield and Dr. Dewey M. Beegle," *The Gordon Review* 8 (Winter 1964–65):108–109; Lindsell, *The Battle for the Bible,* pp. 210–211.

22. Modern neo-evangelicals are often compared with turn-of-the-century liberals H. P. Smith and C. A. Briggs who are said to have exhibited "a sad decline in their faith." Cf. Nicole, "The Inspiration of Scripture: B. B. Warfield and Dr. Dewey M. Beegle," p. 108.

23. John Woodbridge, "History's 'Lessons' and Biblical Inerrancy," *Trinity Journal* 6 (Spring 1977):75.

24. Beegle, *Scripture, Tradition, and Infallibility,* pp. 176ff., 206, 308, 262–263, 276; Stephen T. Davis, *The Debate About the Bible* (Philadelphia: The Westminster Press, 1977), pp. 95, 107, 97, 115–116, 125.

25. Dewey M. Beegle, *The Inspiration of Scripture* (Philadelphia: The Westminster Press, 1963).

26. F. F. Bruce, "Foreword" to Beegle, *Scripture, Tradition, and Infallibility*, pp. 7–10.

27. Beegle, *Scripture, Tradition, and Infallibility*, pp. 206, 258, 309 (Beegle's italics), 262.

28. Davis, *The Debate About the Bible*, p. 126.

29. *Ibid.*, pp. 95ff., 115–120.

30. P. T. Forsyth, quoted in Donald Miller, *The Authority of the Bible* (Grand Rapids: Eerdmans, 1972), p. 62.

31. Davis, *The Debate About the Bible*, p. 126.

32. Cf. James Daane, "The Odds on Inerrancy," *The Reformed Journal* 26 (December 1976):5–6.

33. Pinnock, "The Inerrancy Debate Among the Evangelicals," p. 12.

34. Davis, *The Debate About the Bible*, p. 96.

35. Lindsell, *The Battle for the Bible*, pp. 169, 174ff.

36. Beegle, *The Inspiration of Scripture*, p. 9.

37. Clark Pinnock, "Authority of the Bible," reprint from *His* magazine, p. 4.

38. Clark Pinnock, *A Defense of Biblical Infallibility* (Nutley, N. J.: Presbyterian and Reformed Publishing Company, 1967), pp. 18, 1–10.

39. *Ibid.*, p. 30.

40. Pinnock, "The Inerrancy Debate Among the Evangelicals," p. 12.

41. *Ibid.*

42. Clark Pinnock, "Three Views of the Bible in Contemporary Theology" in *Biblical Authority*, ed. Rogers, p. 62.

43. *Ibid.*, p. 68.

44. Daniel Fuller, "The Nature of Biblical Inerrancy," *Journal of the American Scientific Affiliation* 24 (June 1972):47.

45. Daniel Fuller, *"Let Me Be a Man of One Book"* (Los Angeles: Fuller Evangelistic Association, 1977); cf. Lindsell, *The Battle for the Bible*, p. 115.

46. Fuller, "The Nature of Biblical Inerrancy," pp. 47–49.

47. *Ibid.*, p. 49.

48. Daniel Fuller, "On Revelation and Biblical Authority," *Journal of the Evangelical Theological Society* 16 (Spring 1973):68–69.

49. Statement of Faith of Fuller Theological Seminary, adopted January 31, 1950.

50. Fuller Theological Seminary Statement of Faith, adopted 1970.

51. David Hubbard, "What We Believe and Teach," *Theology, News and Notes* (1976, Special Issue), p. 4.

52. *Ibid.*; Hubbard, "Reflections on Fuller's Theological Position and Role in the Church."

53. Hubbard, "The Current Tensions: Is There a Way Out?", p. 156.

54. Paul Jewett, quoted in "Ad Hoc Committee Clarifies Relationship Between Paul K. Jewett's 'Man as Male and Female' and the Seminary Statement of Faith," *Theology, News and Notes* (1976, Special Issue), pp. 20–22. Cf. Paul Jewett, *Man as Male and Female* (Grand Rapids: Eerdmans, 1975).

55. Jewett, *Man as Male and Female*, pp. 129–149.

56. Lindsell, *The Battle for the Bible*, p. 119.

57. "Ad Hoc Committee Clarifies Relationship Between Paul K. Jewett's 'Man as Male and Female' and the Seminary Statement of Faith," p. 21.

58. *Ibid.*

59. Pinnock, "The Inerrancy Debate Among the Evangelicals." It will be interesting to observe whether Pinnock's move from Regent College, which required its faculty to sign an "inerrancy" statement, to McMaster Divinity College, which has no such stipulation, causes Pinnock to drop the term "inerrant" for something he feels is more appropriate to the Biblical record.

60. Everett Harrison, "The Phenomena of Scripture" in *Revelation and the Bible*, ed. Carl F. H. Henry (Philadelphia: Presbyterian and Reformed Publishing Company, 1958), p. 239.

61. *Ibid.*, pp. 249, 250.

62. Lindsell, *The Battle for the Bible*, pp. 24, 154, 159, 183, 206–211.

63. B. B. Warfield, *The Inspiration and Authority of the Bible* (Philadelphia: Presbyterian and Reformed Publishing Company, 1948), p. 210.

64. Cf. Henry in "The Battle for the Bible: An Interview with Dr. Carl F. H. Henry," p. 3: "the first thing the Bible says about itself is not its inerrancy or its inspiration, but its authority. . . . Just as in the gospels the most important thing is the incarnation, death and resurrection, while the *how* of the incarnation, the virgin birth, lies in the hinterland; so also in respect to the doctrine of Scripture, while inspiration is as clearly taught as the virgin birth, it lies rather in the hinterland."

65. Daane, "The Odds on Inerrancy," p. 6.

66. *Ibid.*

67. "Therefore, illumined by his [the Spirit's] power, we believe neither by our own nor by anyone else's judgment that Scripture is from God; but above human judgment we affirm with utter certainty (just as if we were gazing upon the majesty of God himself) that it has flowed to us from the very mouth of God by the ministry of men. We seek no proofs, no marks of genuineness upon which our judgment may lean; but we subject our judgment and wit to it as to a thing far beyond any guesswork!" John Calvin, *Institutes of the Christian Religion*, trans. Ford Lewis Battles (Philadelphia: The Westminster Press, 1960), I. vii. 5, p. 80. It is important to note that appeal to

the witness of the Spirit is not "subjective and experiential" for Calvin, but objective in its God-givenness. Cf. Geisler, "The Nature of Scripture," p. 34.

68. Lindsell, *The Battle for the Bible,* pp. 169–172.

69. Geoffrey W. Bromiley, "The Inspiration & Authority of Scripture," *Eternity,* August 1970, p. 16.

70. Pinnock, "The Inerrancy Debate Among the Evangelicals," p. 12.

71. Jewett, *Man as Male and Female,* p. 134 (Jewett's italics).

72. Harold Lindsell, "The Infallible Word," *Christianity Today* 16 (August 25, 1972):10.

73. Fuller, "The Nature of Biblical Inerrancy," p. 49.

74. John Calvin, *Commentaries on the Epistle of Paul the Apostle to the Hebrews,* trans. John Owen (Grand Rapids: Eerdmans, 1948), quoted in *ibid.*

75. Jewett, *Man as Male and Female,* p. 138.

Chapter III: The Role of Women in the Church and Family: The Issue of Biblical Hermeneutics

1. Marabel Morgan, *The Total Woman* (Old Tappan, N.J.: Fleming H. Revell, 1973); Virginia R. Mollenkott, *Women, Men, and the Bible* (Nashville: Abingdon, 1977); Helen Andelin, *Fascinating Womanhood* (Santa Barbara, Calif.: Pacific Press, 1963); Don Williams, *The Apostle Paul and Women in the Church* (Van Nuys, Calif.: BIM Publishing Co., 1977); Larry Christenson, *The Christian Family* (Minneapolis: Bethany Fellowship, 1970); Gladys Hunt, *Ms. Means Myself* (Grand Rapids: Erdmans, 1972); Letha Scanzoni and Nancy Hardesty, *All We're Meant to Be* (Waco: Word Books, 1974); Elisabeth Elliot, *Let Me Be a Woman* (Wheaton: Tyndale House, 1976); George W. Knight, III, *The New Testament Teaching on the Role Relationship of Men and Women* (Grand Rapids: Baker Book House, 1977). Note: although Helen Andelin is a Mormon, her book (and workshops) has been widely subscribed to by evangelicals and is thus included here.

2. *New Wine* tried to counter what they felt was an un-Biblical feminism by devoting a whole issue to "The Restoration of Manhood" (October 1975).

3. For example, George W. Knight, III, "Male and Female Related He Them," *Christianity Today* 20 (April 9, 1976):13–17; Winnie Christenson, "What Is a Woman's Role?", *Moody Monthly* 71 (June 1971):82–83; Charles Simpson, "The Home: Heaven or Earth?", *Logos* 4 (September-October 1974):13–15; Virginia R. Mollenkott, "Church Women, Theologians, and the Burden of Proof," *The Reformed Journal* 25 (July-August 1975):18–20 and (September 1975):17–21; Nancy Hardesty, "Women: 2nd Class Citizens?", *Eternity,* January 1971, pp. 14–16, 24–29; David Scaer, "What Did St.

Paul Want?", *His* 33 (May 1976):12ff.; "Beyond the Barriers and the Stereotypes: All We're Meant to Be" (a *Vanguard* interview with Letha Scanzoni and Nancy Hardesty), *Vanguard,* March-April 1975, pp. 13–16; Virginia R. Mollenkott, "A Challenge to Male Interpretation," *Sojourners* 5 (February 1976):20–25.

4. *Daughters of Sarah* prints the following position statement in its pages:

We are Christians; we are also feminists. Some say we cannot be both, but Christianity and feminism for us are inseparable.

DAUGHTERS OF SARAH is our attempt to share our discoveries, our struggles, and our growth as Christian women. We are committed to Scripture and we seek to find in it meaning for our lives. We are rooted in a historical tradition of women who have served God in innumerable ways and we seek guidance from their example. We are convinced that Christianity is relevant to all areas of women's lives today. We seek ways to act out our faith.

5. For example, Thomas Howard and Donald W. Dayton, "A Dialogue on Women, Hierarchy and Equality," *Post American* 4 (May 1975):10; Elisabeth Elliot Leitch, "Feminism or Femininity?", *Cambridge Fish* 5 (Winter 1975–76):2, 6; Carl F. H. Henry, "The Battle of the Sexes," *Christianity Today* 19 (July 4, 1975):45–46; Nancy Hardesty, "Women and Evangelical Christianity" in *The Cross & the Flag,* ed. Robert Clouse, Robert Linder, and Richard Pierard (Carol Stream, Ill.: Creation House, 1972), p. 71.

6. Krister Stendahl, *The Bible and the Role of Women: A Case Study in Hermeneutics,* trans. Emilie Sander (Philadelphia: Fortress Press, 1966).

7. Howard and Dayton, "A Dialogue on Women, Hierarchy and Equality," pp. 12–13.

8. Virginia R. Mollenkott, reply to Sharon Gallagher, *Sojourners* 5 (March 1976):37–38; idem, "A Challenge to Male Interpretation," p. 22.

9. "A Conversation with Virginia Mollenkott," *The Other Side,* May-June 1976, p. 22. Cf. Mollenkott, *Women, Men, and the Bible,* pp. 90–106. Her chapter is entitled "Pauline Contradictions and Biblical Inspiration."

10. Paul Jewett, *Man as Male and Female* (Grand Rapids: Eerdmans, 1975), pp. 134, 138, 118.

11. Cf. Phyllis Alsdurf, "The Role of Women Within the Body of Christ," March 1976, pp. 6–8 (typewritten) for a helpful discussion of Jewett's exegesis.

12. Jewett, *Man as Male and Female,* pp. 112–113.

13. In this regard, Mollenkott acts at cross-purposes with another of her basic hermeneutical principles—that consistency should be assumed if possible. She says: "One of the best guidelines is what theologians call the analogy of faith, or what I call assuming a book hangs

together. In this connection I ought to be willing to give the Bible the same respect I give Homer or *The Divine Comedy* or Milton. So if I find a passage in *Paradise Lost* that seems to run counter to everything else in *Paradise Lost,* I immediately suspect my reading and try to find a reading that is coherent with the rest of it." Unfortunately, Mollenkott then turns to a discussion of women in Scripture and says, "So when I see a few passages that seem to come down on certain members of the human race or seem to humiliate or reject them, I am going to be very slow to say that the vast majority of passages (which say the opposite) are wrong. When we find a passage, a spirit which runs all the way through the Bible—at that point I know which one is for all time and which one for the hardness of our hearts" ("A Conversation with Virginia Mollenkott," pp. 74–75). What escapes Mollenkott is the fact that the hermeneutical principle she enunciates does not suggest dismissing a passage because of "the hardness of our hearts," but rather reevaluating it with fresh, exacting, detailed research seeking a thread by which the "book hangs together."

14. Harold Lindsell, "Egalitarianism and Scriptural Infallibility," *Christianity Today* 20 (March 26, 1976):45–46.
15. Nancy Hardesty, letter in *Christianity Today* 20 (June 4, 1976):25.
16. Stendahl, *The Bible and the Role of Women,* p. 14.
17. G. C. Berkouwer, *Holy Scripture* (Grand Rapids: Eerdmans, 1975), p. 188.
18. Leitch, "Feminism or Femininity?", p. 6.
19. Elliot, "Let Me Be a Woman," p. 22.
20. Elisabeth Elliot, "Why I Oppose the Ordination of Women," *Christianity Today* 19 (June 6, 1975):14. Elliot takes a similar uncritical view of Genesis 2, seeing its intent as being to describe more specifically the chronology of the creation of man and woman (*ibid.,* p. 13). Similarly, Elliot views Paul's admonitions to women about praying and prophesying as "clearly exceptions to the rule of silence" (*ibid.,* p. 14). Cf. "A HIS Interview with Elisabeth Elliot," *His* 34 (January 1978):18–24.
21. Howard and Dayton, "A Dialogue on Women, Hierarchy and Equality," p. 9.
22. C. S. Lewis, "Priestesses in the Church," *God in the Dock* (Grand Rapids: Eerdmans, 1970), pp. 234–239.
23. For example, Elisabeth Elliot's claim that "the pronouns referring to him [God] in Scripture are *without exception masculine*" (Elliot, "Why I Oppose the Ordination of Women," p. 16, emphasis added). Cf. Isaiah 49:15; Matthew 23:37.
24. Berkouwer, *Holy Scripture,* p. 239.
25. Cf. *ibid.,* pp. 213–239.

26. Billy Graham, "Jesus and the Liberated Woman," *Ladies' Home Journal* 87 (December 1970):42.
27. *Ibid.,* p. 114.
28. Graham's "cultural Christianity" finds a strong echo in his wife's comment concerning women's ordination in *Christianity Today:* " 'clergywomen'? I have serious reservations. I think if you study you will find that the finest cooks in the world are men (probably called chefs); the finest couturiers, by and large, are men; the finest musicians are men; the greatest politicians are men; most of our greatest writers are men; most of our greatest athletes are men. You name it, men are superior in all but two areas: women make the best wives and women make the best mothers!" Ruth Graham, "Others Say . . . Women's Ordination," *Christianity Today* 19 (June 6, 1975):32.
29. Kathryn Lindskoog, "Paul's Bad News for Women," *The Other Side,* July–August 1973, p. 11.
30. *Ibid.,* p. 10. It is interesting to notice that one can almost predict a person's stance by her or his delimitation of the relevant text in both 1 Corinthians 14 and Ephesians 5. Is the text to be considered 1 Corinthians 14:34–35, or is the wider context of proper decorum and order necessary to its meaning? Does Ephesians 5:22 begin a new paragraph, or must we begin with Ephesians 5:21 which discusses mutual submission? Cf. George W. Knight, "The New Testament Teaching on the Role Relationship of Male and Female with Special Reference to the Teaching/Ruling Functions in the Church," *Journal of the Evangelical Theological Society* 18 (Spring 1975), and Lindskoog, "Paul's Bad News for Women."
31. Cf. David and Elouise Fraser, "A Biblical View of Women: Demythologizing Sexegesis," *Theology, News and Notes* 21 (June 1975):18. The Frasers similarly ignore Paul's advice to the wife in the discussion of Ephesians 5. On the other side, Gladys Hunt, in her discussion of Ephesians 5 which is meant to support a hierarchical understanding of family authority, conveniently ignores Paul's advice to the husband. See Hunt, *Ms. Means Myself,* pp. 97ff.
32. Cf. John Alexander, "Thinking Male: Or How to Hide Behind the Bible," *The Other Side,* July–August 1973, pp. 3–4, 43–47.
33. Scanzoni and Hardesty, *All We're Meant to Be,* pp. 18–19. Cf. "A Conversation with Virginia Mollenkott," p. 73; Howard and Dayton, "A Dialogue on Women, Hierarchy and Equality," p. 14; Jewett, *Man as Male and Female,* pp. 142–147.
34. This is faintly reminiscent of Edward J. Carnell's *The Case for Orthodox Theology,* which argued that some parts of Scripture must take priority over other parts. In particular, the New Testament is to interpret the Old Testament; the epistles are to interpret the Gospels; systematic passages should interpret the incidental; universal, the

local; and didactic, the symbolic. See Edward J. Carnell, "Hermeneutics," *The Case for Orthodox Theology* (Philadelphia: The Westminster Press, 1959), pp. 51–65. It is interesting to note that Carnell finds Romans and Galatians the supreme interpretations of the revelation of God in Christ. Several Biblical feminists similarly find Galatians 3:28 the "theological breakthrough" that is determinative of their interpretation of liberation in Christ. Cf. Jewett, *Man as Male and Female*, p. 144.

35. William L. Lane, "Task Theology: The Transcultural Character of the Gospel," paper presented at the southern sectional meeting of the Evangelical Theological Society, Bowling Green, Kentucky, February 1976.

36. Cf. James W. Jones, "Task Theology and Dogmatic Theology," Spring 1976 (typewritten).

37. A classic instance of this danger is Gerhard von Rad's *Old Testament Theology*, which reduces the message of Wisdom literature to that of a response to Heilsgeschichte. In *Wisdom in Israel*, a later volume, von Rad tries to rectify this error.

38. Paul Holmer, "Contemporary Evangelical Faith" in *The Evangelicals*, ed. David F. Wells and John D. Woodbridge (Nashville: Abingdon, 1975), p. 77.

39. A variation on the "locus classicus" approach is the desire to judge Scripture by "what Jesus said and did" ("A Conversation with Virginia Mollenkott," p. 75). What is not made explicit is the assumed identification of Jesus with a certain theological formulation of women's place. Aside from the fact that this merely shifts the problem from discerning what the "epistles" mean to finding what the "Gospels" say, it also reflects the same propensity for a "canon within a canon." It is now Christology, rather than systematics, that is thought normative over the Biblical witness. Cf. Scanzoni and Hardesty, *All We're Meant to Be*, pp. 85–87.

40. Harold Lindsell, *The World, the Flesh, and the Devil* (Washington, D. C.: Canon Press, 1973), pp. 146–150.

41. *Ibid.*, p. 132.

42. Knight, "The New Testament Teaching on the Role Relationship of Male and Female with Special Reference to the Teaching/Ruling Functions in the Church," p. 89.

43. Hunt, *Ms. Means Myself*, p. 12.

44. *Ibid.*, pp. 25–39.

45. *Ibid.*, pp. 90–103.

46. Rey O'Day Mawson, "Why All the Fuss About Language?", *Post American* 3 (August–September 1974):16.

47. J. Massyngberde Ford, "Biblical Material Relevant to the Ordination of Women," *Journal of Ecumenical Studies* 10 (Fall 1973):677, notes

that in the LXX the masculine form *prostates* (fem. *prostatis*) is used of stewards (1 Chron. 27:31), officers (1 Chron. 29:6; 2 Chron. 8:10), governors (1 Esd. 2:12; 2 Macc. 3:4). See Scanzoni and Hardesty, *All We're Meant to Be,* p. 217.

48. Howard and Dayton, "A Dialogue on Women, Hierarchy and Equality," p. 14.

49. Lucille Sider Dayton, "The Feminist Movement and Scripture," *Post American* 3 (August–September 1974):10; Mollenkott, *Women, Men, and the Bible,* pp. 9–33.

50. Scanzoni and Hardesty, *All We're Meant to Be,* p. 100.

51. Knight, "Male and Female Related He Them," p. 14.

52. Knight, "The New Testament Teaching on the Role Relationship of Male and Female with Special Reference to the Teaching/Ruling Functions in the Church," p. 89. For a more helpful model, see Williams, *The Apostle Paul and Women in the Church.* In this book Williams considers all of the Pauline references to women, placing them first within their immediate context in the epistles.

53. Russell Prohl, *Woman in the Church* (Grand Rapids: Eerdmans, 1957), pp. 20–23.

54. Cf. Marchiene Vroon-Rienstra, "Women and the Church," *Dialogue,* January 1977, pp. 7–11.

55. Paul Jewett has an excellent, brief review of several classic theological statements regarding women in his book *Man as Male and Female,* pp. 61–82.

56. Knight, "The New Testament Teaching on the Role Relationship of Male and Female with Special Reference to the Teaching/Ruling Functions in the Church"; John Reumann, "What in Scripture Speaks to the Ordination of Women?", *Concordia Theological Monthly* 44 (January 1973); Donald Dayton and Lucille Sider Dayton, "Women as Preachers: Evangelical Precedents," *Christianity Today* 19 (May 23, 1975); Lindsell, *The World, the Flesh, and the Devil.*

57. Even with the sharing of insights through commentaries and books, biases remain. To give one further example, Dorothy Pape provides us her 370–page personal journey through the New Testament, *In Search of God's Ideal Woman* (Downers Grove, Ill.: Inter-Varsity Press, 1976). She quotes commentators widely and provides strong evidence against a traditionalist position. But she nevertheless claims that her book is "not meant as a brief for women ministers" (p. 45). Rather, it is simply a defense of "great women missionaries [who] were not necessarily out of God's will" in their teaching and preaching and evangelizing (p. 207). It is hardly surprising to discover Pape is herself a missionary out of a tradition in which women have historically been denied ordination. Such an example, though more

obvious than some, should remind us all of the need for a basic
humility in our claims to let Scripture speak authoritatively. We
must be willing always to be corrected and then to act on what we
hear.

Chapter IV: Evangelical Social Ethics: The Use of One's Theological Tradition

1. Vernon Grounds, *Evangelicalism and Social Responsibility* (Scottdale, Pa.: Herald Press, 1969), pp. 4–6.
2. David Moberg, *The Great Reversal: Evangelism Versus Social Concern* (Philadelphia: Lippincott, 1972), p. 41.
3. William Brenton Greene, Jr., "The Church and the Social Question," *Princeton Theological Review,* July 1912, pp. 377–398.
4. Billy Graham, *World Aflame* (Garden City, N.Y.: Doubleday, 1965), pp. 172–173; John W. Montgomery, "Evangelical Social Responsibility" in *Our Society in Turmoil,* ed. Gary R. Collins (Carol Stream, Ill.: Creation House, 1971), p. 15; Robert D. Linder and Richard V. Pierard, *Politics: A Case for Christian Action* (Downers Grove, Ill.: Inter-Varsity Press, 1973), p. 127; Mark Hatfield, *Between a Rock and a Hard Place* (Waco: Word Books, 1976), p. 68; Sherwood Wirt, *The Social Conscience of the Evangelical* (New York: Harper & Row, 1968), p. 154; Bill Bright, "Foreword" to *Save America* by H. Edward Rowe (Old Tappan, N. J.: Fleming H. Revell, 1976), p. 13; Richard Quebedeaux, *The Young Evangelicals* (New York: Harper & Row, 1974), p. 99.
5. Billy Graham, *Peace with God* (Garden City, N.Y.: Doubleday, 1953), p. 190.
6. Carl F. H. Henry, *The Uneasy Conscience of Modern Fundamentalism* (Grand Rapids: Eerdmans, 1947), pp. 10, 26, 68.
7. Graham, *Peace with God,* p. 190.
8. Montgomery, "Evangelical Social Responsibility," p. 15.
9. Carl F. H. Henry, "Strife Over Social Concerns: Sixth in the Series 'Evangelicals in Search of Identity'," *Christianity Today* 20 (June 4, 1976):32.
10. Judy Brown Hull, "In Praise of Holding Together," *Sojourners* 6 (February 1977):35.
11. Cf. Isaac Rottenberg, "The Shape of the Church's Social-Economic Witness," *The Reformed Journal* 27 (May 1977):16–21; Jim Wallis, "What Does Washington Have to Say to Grand Rapids?", *Sojourners* 6 (July 1977):3–4; Nicholas P. Wolterstorff, "How Does Grand Rapids Reply to Washington?", *The Reformed Journal* 27 (October 1977):10–14; Isaac Rottenberg, "Dimensions of the Kingdom: A Dialogue with 'Sojourners'," *The Reformed Journal* 27 (November 1977):17–21.
12. Evangelicals share a common commitment to a personal experience with

Christ as Lord and to the Bible as authoritative, but they are perhaps as diverse as Christendom itself as to their theological roots. Other prominent traditions include Lutherans, Pentecostals, and a rising number of Roman Catholics.

13. Quoted in "The Stand at Lausanne," *Moody Monthly* 74 (September 1974):21.

14. Howard Whaley, "The Church, the World Wars," *Moody Monthly* 76 (October 1976):118–125.

15. George Sweeting, "We Need a Spiritual Awakening," *Moody Monthly* 72 (April 1972):20–21, 105.

16. George Sweeting, "America, Right oı Wrong?" *Moody Monthly* 74 (August 1974):3.

17. Cf. "Church Flab and the Energy Crisis," *Moody Monthly* 74 (March 1974):20; "The Blessings of Not Having It So Good," *Moody Monthly* 75 (February 1975):19; "A Time to Give Thanks," *Moody Monthly* 73 (December 1973):21; "Problems: The People's Choice," *Moody Monthly* 75 (March 1975):21.

18. Carl F. H. Henry, "Evangelicals in the Social Struggle," *Christianity Today* 10 (October 8, 1965):3–11; idem, *Aspects of Christian Social Ethics* (Grand Rapids: Eerdmans, 1964).

19. "How Did We Get There?", *Christianity Today* 17 (November 24, 1972):29.

20. "Watergate and Religion," *Christianity Today* 17 (August 31, 1973):28.

21. "The Marxist Never-Never-Land," *Christianity Today* 19 (December 20, 1974):20. Cf. "The WCC at Nairobi: Twenty-Seven Years Later," *Christianity Today* 19 (September 12, 1975):45.

22. "Some Things Are Always Wrong," *Christianity Today* 19 (March 12, 1976):38.

23. Cf. "A UN Seat for Christians?", *Christianity Today* 19 (November 8, 1974):29.

24. "Why Are People Starving?", *Christianity Today* 19 (October 25, 1974): 35. Cf. "Counting the Cost of Giving," *Christianity Today* 20 (January 30, 1976):21.

25. "Where Is Tomorrow's Food?", *Christianity Today* 18 (September 13, 1974):53.

26. "Provoking to Good Works," *Christianity Today* 18 (December 21, 1973):23.

27. Cf. "The Place to Start," *Christianity Today* 18 (September 27, 1974): 36–37, which denies Mark Hatfield's claim that "the present economic and political system of our society is unacceptable."

28. "Plain Talk on Viet Nam," *Christianity Today* 16 (May 26, 1972):27.

29. Lewis Smedes, "A Senator on Sin," *The Reformed Journal* 20 (July–August 1970):4–5.

30. *Ibid.*

31. Cf. Lewis Smedes, "Pandering and Pornography," *The Reformed Jour-*

nal 20 (April 1969):5; Richard Mouw, "The Church and Social Specifics," *The Reformed Journal* 19 (July–August 1969):2–4.

32. Lewis Smedes, "Should the Church Speak on Political Issues?", *Eternity,* December 1967, p. 24.

33. Lewis Smedes, "Who Speaks for the Church, and How?", *The Reformed Journal* 17 (December 1967):6.

34. Lewis Smedes, "Comments on Vietnam," *The Reformed Journal* 17 (July–August 1967):6–7. Fellow editor and faculty colleague James Daane is more willing than Smedes to directly address social and public policy. In a review of Sherwood Wirt's influential book *The Social Conscience of an Evangelical* in *The Reformed Journal* 18 (May–June 1968):19, Daane argues that churches can make specific social and political announcements for three reasons: (1) Protestants are not committed to belief in an infallible church and therefore can risk error. They do this in their preaching. Why not in their social involvement? (2) When individual Christians speak to public issues, Christ's church is identified with them. If individuals can nevertheless represent (and misrepresent) Christ in the public arena, why not the corporate church as well? (3) When individuals speak, they are willy-nilly acting corporately, for the Christian fellowship *is* one body. Doesn't the church have an equal right to that of individual Christians to make a corporate statement?

35. Lewis Smedes, "Where Do We Differ?", *The Reformed Journal* 16 (May–June 1966):10.

36. *Ibid.*, p. 9.

37. Lewis Smedes, "The Evangelicals and the Social Question," *The Reformed Journal* 16 (February 1966):12.

38. Lewis Smedes, "Suffering: The Christian Style of Life," *The Reformed Journal* 19 (February 1969):11–13.

39. Lewis Smedes, "A Modest Proposal to Reform the World," *The Reformed Journal* 21 (February 1971):14.

40. Smedes, "Who Speaks for the Church, and How?", p. 7.

41. Jim Wallis, "The New Community," *Post American* 2 (September–October 1973):1.

42. Jim Wallis, "Interview: Carl Henry on Evangelical Identity," *Sojourners* 5 (April 1976):29.

43. Wallis, "What Does Washington Have to Say to Grand Rapids?", p. 4.

44. Wallis, "Interview: Carl Henry on Evangelical Identity," p. 30.

45. *Ibid.*

46. Cf. Jim Wallis, *Agenda for Biblical People* (New York: Harper & Row, 1976), p. 134.

47. Wallis, "What Does Washington Have to Say to Grand Rapids?", p. 4.

48. Jim Wallis, "The Move to Washington, D. C.," *Post American* 4 (August–September 1975):4.

49. "Capital Flight," *Newsweek,* 7 February 1977, p. 77. Copyright 1977 by Newsweek, Inc. All rights reserved. Reprinted by permission.

50. Rus Walton, *One Nation Under God* (Washington, D. C.: Third Century Publishers, 1975).

51. David O. Moberg, *Inasmuch: Christian Social Responsibility in the Twentieth Century* (Grand Rapids: Eerdmans, 1965).

52. Mark Hatfield, *Between a Rock and a Hard Place.*

53. Wallis, "What Does Washington Have to Say to Grand Rapids?", p. 4.

54. Hull, "In Praise of Holding Together," p. 35.

55. Moberg, *Inasmuch,* p. 98.

56. Jacques Ellul, *The Theological Foundation of Law* (Garden City, N. Y.: Doubleday, 1960), p. 86; Emil Brunner, *Justice and the Social Order* (New York: Harper and Brothers, 1945), p. 1; cf. James Booker, "Dürrenmatt's Concept of Justice," *Christian Scholars Review* 6 (November 4, 1977):317–325.

57. Foy Valentine, "Engagement—The Christian's Agenda" in *The Chicago Declaration,* ed. Ronald Sider (Carol Stream, Ill.: Creation House, 1974), pp. 67–68.

58. Cf. Ron Sider, "Is God Really on the Side of the Poor?", *Sojourners* 6 (October 1977):11–14; Stephen Charles Mott, "Egalitarian Aspects of the Biblical Theory of Justice," *Selected Papers of the American Society of Christian Ethics: 1978.*

59. Henry, "Evangelicals in the Social Struggle," p. 6.

60. Hatfield, *Between a Rock and a Hard Place,* pp. 131–150.

61. Moberg, *Inasmuch,* p. 39; cf. pp. 29–58.

62. Walton, *One Nation Under God,* p. 64.

63. Cf. Paul Ramsey, *Basic Christian Ethics* (New York: Charles Scribner's Sons, 1950), pp. 2–3.

64. *Ibid.,* pp. 4–5.

65. Wallis, "Interview: Carl Henry on Evangelical Identity," p. 32.

66. Smedes, "Where Do We Differ?", p. 10.

67. Carl F. H. Henry, quoted in "Interview: Carl Henry on Evangelical Identity," p. 32.

68. Timothy L. Smith, *Revivalism and Social Reform in Mid-Nineteenth Century America* (New York: Abingdon, 1957).

69. Wallis, "What Does Washington Have to Say to Grand Rapids?", p. 3.

70. Wallis, *Agenda for Biblical People,* p. 132.

71. *Ibid.,* p. 102.

72. Paul B. Henry, "Love, Power and Justice," *The Christian Century* 94 (November 23, 1977):1089.

73. Wes Michaelson, quoted in "Interview: Carl Henry on Evangelical Identity," p. 30; cf. Wallis, *Agenda for Biblical People,* p. 123.

74. Wolterstorff, "How Does Grand Rapids Reply to Washington?", p. 13.

75. *Ibid.*

76. Billy Graham, "Why Lausanne?", mimeographed address of July 16, 1974, p. 12, quoted in Ronald Sider, "Evangelism, Salvation and Social Justice: Definitions and Interrelationships," *International Review of Mission* 64 (July 1975):251–252. In the discussion of evangelism and social justice, I find myself in general agreement with Sider's formulations and have been influenced by them.

77. John Yoder, *The Politics of Jesus* (Grand Rapids: Eerdmans, 1972), p. 153.

78. Samuel Escobar, "Evangelism and Man's Search for Freedom, Justice and Fulfillment" in *Let the Earth Hear His Voice,* ed. J. D. Douglas (Minneapolis: World Wide Publications, 1975), p. 311.

79. Quebedeaux, *The Young Evangelicals,* p. 97; cf. pp. 86–135.

80. Escobar, "Evangelism and Man's Search for Freedom, Justice and Fulfillment," p. 316.

Chapter V: Homosexuality and the Evangelical: The Influence of Contemporary Culture

1. "Religious Leaders: A Glance Back, a Look Forward," *Christianity Today* 22 (January 13, 1978):30.

2. *Motive* 32 (Nos. 1 and 2, 1972).

3. *Trends* 5 (July-August 1973).

4. "The Church and Homosexuality: A Preliminary Study," Office of the Stated Clerk, The Presbyterian Church in the United States, 1977, p. 28.

5. Current-day theological discussion can perhaps be said to have begun with Derrick Sherwin Bailey, *Homosexuality and the Western Christian Tradition* (London: Longmans, Green and Co., 1955). Other noteworthy studies include Robert Wood, *Christ and the Homosexual* (New York: Vantage Press, 1960); Helmut Thielicke, *The Ethics of Sex,* trans. John Doberstein (New York: Harper & Row, 1964); H. Kimball Jones, *Toward a Christian Understanding of the Homosexual* (New York: Association Press, 1966); *The Same Sex: An Appraisal of Homosexuality,* ed. Ralph Weltge (Philadelphia: United Church Press, 1969); W. Norman Pittenger, *Time for Consent: A Christian's Approach to Homosexuality* (London: SCM Press, 1970); *Is Gay Good?: Ethics, Theology, and Homosexuality,* ed. W. Dwight Oberholtzer (Philadelphia: The Westminster Press, 1971); Troy Perry, *The Lord Is My Shepherd and He Knows I'm Gay* (Los Angeles: Nash Publishing Co., 1972); Alex Davidson, *The Returns of Love: A Contemporary Christian View of Homosexuality* (Downers Grove, Ill.: Inter-Varsity Press, 1971); Barbara Evans, *Joy!* (Carol Stream, Ill.: Creation House, 1973); *Loving Women/Loving Men: Gay Liberation and the Church,* ed. Sally Gearhart and William R. Johnson (San Francisco: Glide Publications, 1974); Clinton Jones, *Homosexuality and Counseling* (Philadelphia: Fortress Press, 1974);

John J. McNeill, *The Church and the Homosexual* (Kansas City, Kans.: Sheed Andrews and McMeel, 1976); Lewis Smedes, *Sex for Christians* (Grand Rapids: Eerdmans, 1976); David Field, *The Homosexual Way—A Christian Option?* (Bramcote, Nottingham: Grove Books, 1976); John White, *Eros Defiled: The Christian and Sexual Sin* (Downers Grove, Ill.: Inter-Varsity Press, 1977); Letha Scanzoni and Virginia R. Mollenkott, *Is the Homosexual My Neighbor?* (New York: Harper & Row, 1978); Don Williams, *The Bond That Breaks: Will Homosexuality Split the Church?* (Los Angeles: BIM Publishing Co., 1978); Jerry Kirk, *The Homosexual Crisis in the Mainline Church* (Nashville: Nelson, 1978); Greg Bahnsen, *Homosexuality: A Biblical View* (Grand Rapids: Baker Book House, 1978); Richard Lovelace, *The Church and Homosexuality* (Old Tappan, N. J.: Fleming H. Revell, 1978).

6. Richard Lovelace, "The Active Homosexual Lifestyle and the Church," *Church & Society* 67 (May-June 1977):37.

7. "What You Think About the Christian in Today's World," *Christian Herald* 101 (January 1978):29.

8. *McCall's,* quoted in *Record* (Newsletter of Evangelicals Concerned, Inc.), Spring 1978.

9. Cf. *His* 38 (February 1978); "Behind Closet Doors: The Door Looks at Homosexuality," *The Wittenburg Door* 39 (October-November 1977); "A Biblical Perspective on Homosexuality and Its Healing," *Journal of the American Scientific Affiliation* 29 (September 1977): 103–110; Lynn Buzzard, "How Gray Is Gay?", *Eternity,* April 1977, pp. 34–37, 42, 44, 46; Don Williams, "Shall We Revise the Homosexual Ethic?", *Eternity,* May 1978, pp. 46–48; Virginia R. Mollenkott and Letha Scanzoni, and John Ostwalt, "Homosexuality: 2 Perspectives," *Daughters of Sarah* 3 (November-December 1977):3–7; Lewis Smedes, "Homosexuality: Sorting Out the Issues," *The Reformed Journal* 28 (January 1978):9–12; Letha Scanzoni, "On Homosexuality: A Response to Smedes," *The Reformed Journal* 28 (May 1978):7–12; Bennett J. Sims, "Sex and Homosexuality," *Christianity Today* 22 (February 24, 1978):23–30; "An Historic Dialogue . . . Homosexuality: A Gift from God?", *Inspiration* 1 (1977): 83–88, 108, 110, 112; Kay Oliver and Wayne Christianson, "Unhappily 'Gay': From the Closet to the Front Page," *Moody Monthly* 78 (January 1978):62–68; Don Marty, "The Church and Homosexuals," *Christian Herald* 101 (January 1978):42–49; Virginia R. Mollenkott and Letha Scanzoni, "Homosexuality: It's Not as Simple as We Think," *Faith at Work* 91 (April 1978):8–10, 18; Don Williams, "Gay Ordination: A Personal Reflection," *Radix* 9 (March-April 1978):21; and *The Other Side,* June 1978.

10. Chris Glaser, "A Newly Revealed Christian Experience," *Church & Society* 67 (May-June 1977):5.

11. William Muehl and William Johnson, "Issues Raised by Homosexuality," *Raising the Issues* (materials distributed as Packet 1, Task Force to Study Homosexuality, United Presbyterian Church), p. 4.
12. Letter from Paul Gebhard to R. Adam DeBaugh, February 10, 1978. Used by permission.
13. For example, Buzzard, "How Gray Is Gay?"; Michael Campion and Alfred Barrow, "When Was the Last Time You Hugged a Homosexual?", *Journal of the American Scientific Affiliation* 29 (September 1977):103–106; Ben Patterson and Kirt Anderson, "A Belated Answer," *The Wittenburg Door* 39 (October-November 1977):18–19, 22–25; Mollenkott and Scanzoni, "Homosexuality: It's Not as Simple as We Think"; Oliver and Christianson, "Unhappily 'Gay': From the Closet to the Front Page"; Williams, *The Bond That Breaks.*
14. "Playboy Interview: Anita Bryant," *Playboy* 25 (May 1978):85.
15. Alan Bell and Martin Weinberg, *Homosexualities: A Study of Diversity Among Men & Women* (New York: Simon and Schuster, 1978).
16. *Medical Aspects of Human Sexuality,* November 1977, quoted in Williams, "Shall We Revise the Homosexual Ethic?", p. 47.
17. Ralph Blair, *Etiological and Treatment Literature on Homosexuality* (New York: Homosexual Community Counseling Center, 1972), p. 24.
18. John Money, quoted in *Determinants of Human Sexual Behavior,* ed. G. Winokur (Springfield, Ill.: Thomas, 1963), quoted in Ralph Blair, *Holier-Than-Thou Hocus-Pocus & Homosexuality* (New York: Homosexual Community Counseling Center, 1977), p. 17.
19. James B. Nelson, "Homosexuality and the Church," *Christianity and Crisis* 37 (April 4, 1977):65–68.
20. Jerry Falwell, quoted in "Battle Over Gay Rights," *Newsweek,* 6 June 1977, p. 22. Copyright 1977 by Newsweek, Inc. All rights reserved. Reprinted by permission.
21. Jack Wyrtzen, quoted *ibid.*
22. Quoted in Ralph Blair, *An Evangelical Look at Homosexuality* (New York: Homosexual Community Counseling Center, 1977), p. 2; "Playboy Interview: Anita Bryant," pp. 76, 78.
23. Quoted in Lovelace, *The Church and Homosexuality,* p. 21.
24. *Ibid.,* p. 87.
25. *Ibid.,* p. 106 (Lovelace's italics).
26. Williams, *The Bond That Breaks,* p. 103.
27. *Ibid.,* pp. 110, 109.
28. *Ibid.,* p. 84.
29. *Ibid.,* p. 118.
30. Thielicke, *The Ethics of Sex,* p. 271.
31. *Ibid.,* p. 281.
32. *Ibid.,* p. 285.

33. Smedes, *Sex for Christians,* p. 70.
34. *Ibid.,* p. 63.
35. *Ibid.,* p. 70.
36. *Ibid.,* p. 73.
37. *Ibid.,* p. 67; cf. Thielicke, *The Ethics of Sex,* p. 281.
38. Scanzoni and Mollenkott, *Is the Homosexual My Neighbor?,* pp. 111, 71, 72.
39. *Ibid.,* p. 129.
40. Williams, "Shall We Revise the Homosexual Ethic?", p. 47.
41. Tim Stafford, "Issue of the Year," *Christianity Today* 22 (May 5, 1978): 36.
42. Kay Lindskoog, review of *Is the Homosexual My Neighbor?* (by Scanzoni and Mollenkott) in *The Wittenburg Door* 39 (October-November 1977):36.
43. Lovelace, *The Church and Homosexuality,* p. 85.
44. Williams, *The Bond That Breaks,* pp. 128–129.
45. David Hubbard, "Homosexuality: Why Can't I Love the Way I Want?" in *God Speaks to the Moral Dilemmas of Our Day* (Los Angeles: Fuller Evangelistic Association, 1977), p. 11.
46. Scanzoni, "On Homosexuality: A Response to Smedes," p. 8.
47. Helmut Thielicke, *The Evangelical Faith* (Grand Rapids: Eerdmans, 1974), p. 127.
48. Ralph Blair, letter to the editor, *Eternity,* July 1977, p. 56 (Blair's italics).
49. Lovelace, *The Church and Homosexuality,* p. 147.
50. E. Mansell Pattison, "Positive Though Inaccurate" (response to Campion and Barrow, "When Was the Last Time You Hugged a Homosexual?") in *Journal of the American Scientific Affiliation* 29 (September 1977):107.
51. Oliver and Christianson, "Unhappily 'Gay': From the Closet to the Front Page," p. 65.
52. Sims, "Sex and Homosexuality," p. 29.
53. Scanzoni, "On Homosexuality: A Response to Smedes," p. 10.
54. Dietrich Bonhoeffer, *Ethics* (New York: Macmillan, 1955), p. 244.
55. Williams, *The Bond That Breaks,* p. 117.
56. Letha Scanzoni, "Changing Family Patterns," *Radix* 8 (May-June 1977):10.
57. Stafford, "Issue of the Year," p. 36.
58. White, *Eros Defiled: The Christian and Sexual Sin,* p. 113.

Chapter VI: Constructive Evangelical Theology

1. James Barr, *Fundamentalism* (London: SCM Press, 1977), p. 187.
2. David Hubbard, "The Future of Evangelicalism," given at a colloquium at Conservative Baptist Theological Seminary, Denver, Colorado, 1977 (manuscript of taped remarks).
3. *Ibid.*

4. David Hubbard, "The Current Tensions: Is There a Way Out?" in *Biblical Authority*, ed. Jack Rogers (Waco: Word Books, 1977), p. 178.

5. G. C. Berkouwer, *Holy Scripture* (Grand Rapids: Eerdmans, 1975), p. 137. Cf. Letha Scanzoni and Virginia R. Mollenkott, *Is the Homosexual My Neighbor?* (New York: Harper & Row, 1978), pp. 20–21.

6. Berkouwer, *Holy Scripture,* p. 137.

7. Karl Barth, quoted in Rudolf Bultmann's introduction to Adolf von Harnack's *What Is Christianity?* (New York: Harper & Row, 1957), p. ix.

8. Bernard Lonergan, *Method in Theology* (New York: Herder and Herder, 1972), p. xi.

9. John H. Leith, "The Bible and Theology," *Interpretation* 30 (July 1976): 233. I am indebted in what follows to this article, although its conclusions move in a different direction from my own.

10. Joseph Sittler, *Nature and Grace* (Philadelphia: Fortress Press, 1972), p. 20, quoted *ibid.*

11. Barth, quoted in Bultmann's introduction to von Harnack's *What Is Christianity?,* p. ix.

12. Berkouwer, *Holy Scripture,* pp. 108–109.

13. Cf. Robert McAfee Brown, *The Pseudonyms of God* (Philadelphia: The Westminster Press, 1972), pp. 19–22.

14. Hubbard, "The Current Tensions: Is There a Way Out?", p. 168.

15. Karl Barth, "The Preface to the Second Edition," *The Epistle to the Romans* (New York: Oxford University Press, 1968), p. 7.

16. John Robertson, quoted in Robert McAfee Brown, "Diversity and Inclusiveness," *Church & Society* 67 (May-June 1977):55.

17. Leith, "The Bible and Theology," p. 239.

18. John Calvin, *Institutes of the Christian Religion,* Volume I (II. ii. 15), ed. John T. McNeill (Philadelphia: The Westminster Press, 1960), p. 273.

19. Brown, *The Pseudonyms of God,* p. 99.

20. *Ibid.,* p. 35.

21. Brown, "Diversity and Inclusiveness," p. 56.

22. Richard Lovelace, *The Church and Homosexuality* (Old Tappan, N. J.: Fleming H. Revell, 1978), p. 5.

23. Calvin, *Institutes of the Christian Religion,* Volume I (I. xiv. 4), p. 164.

24. Karl Barth, *Evangelical Theology: An Introduction* (New York: Doubleday, 1964), p. 160, quoted in Leith, "The Bible and Theology," p. 236.

25. Karl Barth, *Antwort, Karl Barth zum siebzigsten Geburtstag* (Zollikon-Zurich: Evangelischer Verlag, 1956), p. 895, quoted in and translated by Brown, *The Pseudonyms of God,* p. 22.